# PLAYER OF LIFE

---

*Basic Knowledge You Will Need to Become an Effective Player of Life in This New World*

Ivory Ledet

Published by:

**Champions Life Family Church**

**Jeanerette, LA**

Copyright © 2020 by Ivory Ledet



ISBN# 978-1-7923-5430-4 (paperback)

ISBN# 978-1-7923-5431-1 (e-book)

Library of Congress Cataloging-in-Publication Data is available upon request.

All scripture is taken or paraphrased from the King James Version of the Bible.

Published by:

**Champions Life Family Church**

**Post Office Box 586**

**Jeanerette, La 70544**

# CONTENT

## Contents - *Continued*

# FOREWORD

The world, as we knew it at the end of 2019, is not the same today. And by the end of this Covid 19 pandemic, we will probably not remember what it was like today.

We are experiencing a time now, where panic, fear, and division dominates the world. And many are waiting for this crisis to end that they may return to their normal lives again.

Needless to say, there is no more norm. There will only be disappointment waiting for those looking for the norm we left behind.

Laws are changing to implement safety measures which affects our social life.

Jobs that are closed down, adhering to these laws, cannot come back the same. The new social standards will be in effect with them. Changes for improvement will be seen and instituted. Cuts will be made. And some jobs may not even come back.

Schools will change to allow for new safety measures. Education will change to reflect the new history.

The way we shop, and the way we visit, will change. And we cannot even expect the churches to remain the same.

Everything is in chaos now, and the only thing that can come from chaos is order. Either government and society will set a new order, or we will find order in the chaos. But in either case, life can never be the same again. Even sitting around and being away from our normal life is making us forget what was normal.

Everything is becoming new, and with all this newness, the old ways will not be able to find a connecting point. No matter how effective the thing we used to do was, there will probably be no connecting point for it in the new world.

Will all of this be good, or will it be bad? Who knows?

There are several different types of people involved here. There are those who are sitting around waiting for the norm to return. Then there are those who are sitting around theorizing conspiracies without planning how to be self-reliant against or through them.

There are also those who *are* planning. One group of individuals planning and preparing for their personal betterment when the norm returns, and the other group preparing to instate a new norm that would only benefit them as an elite group. Where will you fit in all this?

Are we at the mercy of the world's order, or is there another way?

This book, **"Player Of Life"** contains the answers that you may be looking for.

Yes!  There is another way.  It is a way of being in the world, but not of the world.  It presents the way of living life the way it was created to be lived.

Whether we understand this or not, life was not created to be predicated upon someone else's leading or movement.  We were created to have life any way we choose, from an urbanite, even to the opposite as a hermit.

We believe the first thing to be understood about life is that, God does not make mistakes, nor has he ever made anything flawed.  Everything is, for the purpose that it is.  And life was created for the expressing and experiencing of anything we desire.

If this is the case, then there must be provisions in place, to make any and everything happen as we choose.

Yes!  There is.  And those provisions come in the form of knowledge.  Knowledge of what the world is, and how it operates.  Knowledge of self.  Knowledge of purpose.  And knowledge of God.  All of which are needful to operate effectively in this world.

There is nothing new.  It is information that has always been and will always be.  Many people have this knowledge and are using it effectively.  But this book is for those whom it has been literally hidden from in plain sight.  Those who have been mind-washed to believe that this knowledge is secular and considered to be sacrilege when added to our religious beliefs.

The purpose of this book is to offer the basic understanding of all there is, in short form.  We believe that getting this basic knowledge will cause a paradigm shift in your life, thereby, rendering you independent of the world.  As we said, to be in the world, but not of the world.

**"Player Of Life"** is a short read, but we believe that it is prolific, profound, and positive.

It will open your eyes to what has always been there, but outside of our traditional view of life.

We suggest that you used the system for reading and understanding this book as we used in creating it.  This is a system that we call "L.E.S.S".  It is the acronym for Logic, Experience, Science, and Scripture.  Individually, either of these tools' trumps tradition any day.  But when combined as a body, it can draw out nothing else but truth and understanding.  And this is where purposeful life meets its birth.

So, enjoy the reading of this book, while it takes you into a new and different and effective way of life.

A note to remember:  This book is written from a Christian perspective only because I am a Christian and can only compare it effectively from this point of view.  However, this is not at all, about religion.  Where religious ways are mentioned, it is simply used to explain something of importance that I cannot explain any other way.

All forms of religions are respected, and no form of debasing or proselytizing is intended.

Things that are said, had to be said, to cause or encourage the reader to think outside of the box.

Enjoy the read.

# You Need Your Own Perception of God

Everyone believes there is supremacy in the universe, yet, it is obvious, everyone does not believe that it is the god celebrated in their culture.

While the most will accept the God of their culture, it is accepted with a few grains of salt for easier swallowing. Their idea of God is called religion. However, the changes for acceptation of either of the many forms of religion, creates a problem for the sincere seeker.

Now, he knows not, which God to expose his opened mind to, because he does not know which version of God is the truth he should accept.

For reasons such as this one, we believe that every man needs to know God for himself, and for his own peace and guilt-free living in this world.

However, the only way to know God for yourself is to view him outside of another person's perception of Him.

*Perceptions*

Other people's perception of God began the moment the first words were recorded concerning the knowledge or revelation of him.

And of course, we know, all revelations are interpreted according to the perception of the interpreter.

Perception can be defined as, "The way one sees a thing".  Each perception is based upon the culture, environment, and biases of the interpreter.

We have the Tanakh because of the culture of the Jews. The Veda, the Bhagavad Gita, and the Upanishads are based upon the Eastern Indian or Hindu culture, and the Quran is based upon the Arab or Mid-Eastern culture. There are many more, like the Christian Bible, which includes the Torah from the Jewish Tanakh and the New Testament writings based upon Greco-Roman culture, then the Tao Te Ching, based upon the Chinese or Far Eastern culture.

Religions are not derived from God, but man's interpretation of these culture based Holy Writings; and denominations are birth from these religions to fit the culture and environment of the regions.

All of them are right for the believer, even though they are interpreted differently.  All the Interpreters who received revelation, understood their revelation of God well enough to be inspired to write it, but could only interpret it in the light of their culture.

Their revelations were correct, but they could not understand it, or explain it, outside of the realm of their present knowledge of service toward their God.  This is the only channel they could pass it through.  It was all they could associate it with.  This was their highest; they knew nothing greater.  So, each built their new truths upon this, *their* sense of the highest.

For this reason, men are confused.  It is their attempt to compare their cultural teachings to that of another culture, which is different.  One would always consider himself right, and the other, wrong.   From these thoughts came crusades to win over and educate one culture over to the way of the other.

Take, for instance, our familiar Christian religion; it has more denominations than many others.   Perhaps because it is so widespread in the world.

But the problem that this brings is that each denomination thinks itself more righteous than the next, and this brings cultural wars, even in the same region. Therefore, the problems of wars and prejudices of the world are not of the sinners and so-called outliers from the religion, but the religious themselves. Each thinking that their way is the only right way.

Perhaps this is because each have learned their chosen religion (devotional service) but have left off learning and knowing the one God.  Paul said of the Jews, in his letter to the Romans, "I bear them record they have a zeal of God, but not according to knowledge."  They loved the idea of God, but missed *him,* by homing in on their religion.  They worshipped a religion in the name of God, but obviously without God.  "A form of godliness but denying the powers thereof." Folk have come to make religion their god and have left off knowing God.

They have come to believe that if you know your religion, you obviously know God. They, therefore, no longer have a need to seek God.

In Ephesians 4:11-14, Paul is teaching about the gifts that Christ left behind, of Apostles, Prophets, Evangelists, Pastors and Teachers, for the building up of the Church. This he did so that we might learn one understanding of God, and not be tossed to and fro as children, and carried about by every wind of doctrine. According to the 15th verse, this one doctrine is given that we may grow up into the <u>fullness of Christ</u> in all things. This is not referring to Jesus, but into the fullness of our individual lives that are hid in Christ. We are the body of Christ, according to Christianity.

However, this doctrine has been confused with, and somewhat overtaken by the doctrines of "Worship and Devotion toward God". And these doctrines are different for each religion, and changing in each denomination, according to their cultural beliefs. Neither of these can easily fit into another region or environment. But when they sound good, or make more sense to the hearer, then this foreign doctrine is adopted into the Believer's lifestyle, causing confusion and unacceptance in his environment, thus static.

This means that, without your own personal perception of God, you are caught up in an angry sea of waves, tossing you into an unstable assurance of God, self, and thus, your own life.  We seek then, the approval of man, rather than God.

What about yourself?  Are you willing to sacrifice your short, valuable life period of  around 85 to 100 years, to satisfy man, or would you sacrifice your popularity with man, to have the life you desire in your heart; the one that was planned for you before the beginning of time?

The value of having your own perception of God is explosive.

1.  It gives you confidence to boldly operate in and speak of God and life in an assurance that cannot be refuted, because you know that you know that you know.
2.  You will not lose your footing of self-assurance if someone did try to refute what you believe, because now, you have searched, and examined the evidence, and know it for yourself.
3.  You can stand on your own two feet and be independent.  You will become impervious to the things that will cause you to be tossed about by every wind of doctrine.
4.  Your self-assurance and knowledge will be admired and respected, and even feared in some areas, when you are sure of the knowledge you are standing on.

5. Your faith will soar to new heights because you are sure.
6. Your fear will completely disappear, and the chains of bondage will fall off. (*"You will know the truth, and the truth will make you free."*)
7. You will know how to pray, and your prayers will be answered.
8. You will know what God desires of you.

At this point, if you still believe that you know God, and have your *own* personal perception of him, then take this next moment to answer the following questions in a sentence or two. These are three simple questions which have no relevancy now, except to be compared to your knowledge upon finishing the reading of this book.

This will be used as your own personal measurement of your growth after completing the book.

1. Why did God choose to create?

2. What was God's purpose for creating you?

3. Where did you get your self-identity from?

# There is Only One Doorway Left Open to Us to Obtain Our Own Perception of God

God, who desires to be personally known, has already prepared a way for us in the very beginning. In each cultural Holy Book, he left a doorway to a personal knowledge of himself, and all that is. It is so simple that we easily walk by it without seeing it. Or, perhaps, because we are not looking for it.

The Christian Bible begins, ***"In the beginning God created the heaven and the earth."*** The obvious offset of this sentence that would be noticed by the seeker, is the word, "Beginning". It obviously does not have to be there. At any point that God started to create could only be the beginning. Yet the Bible still says, In the beginning God created...", as if he could have possibly created at the end or in the middle of creation.

I have always known the Bible to be precise in its wording unless it is trying to make a particular point. And this stood out like a sore thumb. The statement could have easily been, "When God first began to create..." It would have been easily understood, and perhaps more acceptable.

The word, "Beginning", however, is a marker; it is a line of demarcation set for the seeker.  It is wisdom set there to give us the knowledge or assurance, that just as sure as there is a story of an effect on one side of the beginning, there is the story of the cause of that effect on the other side.  On one side of the line is the story of creation, and the other side, the story of that which was before creation, the cause.  This "Beginning" is our only connection to God, and the only doorway to knowing him.

On the creation side is the universe and all the hosts of it.  On the other side, God alone, since nothing yet had been created.

On the side of creation, from the very beginning of recording, is someone else's perception of God.  But on the other side of the beginning is God alone, and the only doorway to obtaining your own perception of the Almighty.

You must see God for yourself by consciously, logically, viewing the evidence in a neutral way of obtaining your own perception without being guided by the rules, laws, and traditions of religion, only evidence.  You will know then that this understanding is the best you can get, and it will be 100% right for you, and thus, 100% right in the sight of God.  You will then know true righteousness, and your self-confidence and your faith will begin to soar to no end.

The most direct and clearest command in the Bible is, "Seek ye the Lord while he may be found." In another passage it says, "Seek ye the Lord if haply you might feel after him and find him." In the Gospel of Thomas, it is written, "Let him who seek, not stop until he finds."

These are a few among scores of other passages admonishing us to seek until we find the Lord. We might consider this, the only "Must" of the Bible, since without this knowledge of who He is and why he created us, we cannot know how to serve him, let alone, know how to live upon this earth. So, we must seek God to know him, or, choose to exist in the darkness and poverty of ignorance. That is, to be swayed by every wind of doctrine. To live what someone else has decided that we should live.

# GETTING TO KNOW GOD

## *Obtaining Your Own Perception of the Almighty*

To begin, we should understand that when we are daydreaming, worrying, or putting our attention on something somewhere other than where we are, we have literally left the body and the place where we were, to venture in another area for a period of time.  We can confidently say that this happens to us on a daily basis.  Perhaps some of us are aware of it, and perhaps some, not.  Most of us call it, "Daydreaming, or drifting off in your mind."

Well, this is where we want to take you now.  We are asking you to take your consciousness; your mind, back to the line of demarcation, which is the beginning.  This line representing the beginning, is literally the doorway to the knowledge of both sides.  On one side, the beginning of the knowledge of creation, and on the other side, the beginning of the knowledge of God.  Both, clearly accessible without the tainting of someone else's perception.

Let us take a step over into the knowledge of the God before creation. This is a side that very few have ever ventured. These few are called mystics or holy men by the world, because of their pure knowledge of God.

**Warning:** As we go into this place, we want to give you a strict warning: Since you don't know God by your own perception yet, do not profane this place we're entering into, with your pre-ordained thoughts of who God is. Remember, you are going in for evidence to gain knowledge in order to form your own perception of God, and not to present that which you have been taught from someone else's perception. Your pre-ordained thoughts are vanity, and thus, an abomination to God. Caution!!!

## *On the Opposite Side of Creation Was God Alone*

We can say that God was alone because scripture says that he created all things, but he did not create until the beginning.  Since we have stepped over from the beginning, then the beginning has not yet come.

In the beginning he created the heaven and the earth. This was the entire universe.  There was nothing created that was not created at this point.

But before the beginning, there was only God.  There was no heaven, no hell, no angels, no throne, and no Devil.  God was all there is, and therefore, there was not an outside to God, and no material in God, and no such thing as time.

Let us examine this.  If God was in heaven, then heaven would have to have been outside of God to contain him. Since there is not an outside to God, then heaven, as we know it, would not have existed.

If we say there were angels with God, then we would have to say that angels were a part of the "us" and "our" in the creation of man, where God said, "Let us make man in our image, after our likeness."  The exception to this is that man was made in the image of God, and not angels.  Angels are messengers, and if God were One Being, who then, would the angels be delivering messages to.

According to Hebrews 1:13-14, Angels are created beings, made to minister for the inhabitants of the earth.  At this point, angels would not have been needed.

If we say God was on a throne, then we would have to consider the fact that if God were One, who and what would he rule from the throne.  To have throne dominion means to have citizens subject to him, which was impossible since nothing had been created yet.

If we say that God had material to create with, then we would have to ask where the material came from, since there was only the invisible God, who is spirit, mind, consciousness.  There was not an outside to him to find material, and there was nothing created yet.

What about Hell, and the Devil: Who and what would they have been for?

The fact is, before the beginning, there was only God. He was All.

## *Getting A Description of God*

Our Christian Bible says that God is invisible, yet there are drawings and paintings of Him, such as Michelangelo's Sistine Chapel depiction, that we give respect to. But how do the painters know what He looks like?

The many different cultures see Him in their own way; some as the sun, the moon, stone carvings, silver, or gold moldings. Some even see Him as birds, or animals, or a combination of birds, animal, and man.

These are called idols, and are said by Christian scripture, to be an abomination to God. We know that man senses God in his spirit, and because he knows nothing else of God, his description of the Almighty is an idol, in the form of something that can be seen with the naked eyes, or something man can identify with. After all, we do experience things with our senses.

Here in America, and basically in the West, we see God as an elderly Caucasian male with a white beard and white robe, sitting on a throne.

In India, God is seen as an equally male female looking person, with many arms, sitting in a lotus position. He and she are interchangeable in references.

In Ephesus, She is seen with many feeding breasts, like as a mother.

And in Egypt, He is seen as a man "Ra" with an animal head, and "Thoth", a man with a bird head.

These are just a few of the many idols that we have made of God.  And all of them fail us because we see them in the form of creation, and not of the Creator.

Those who see God as a stone, see him as strong, but he cannot move himself, so how can he save them.

Those who worship the gold and silver images, see him as rich, but he cannot support them, because his only worth is what they put of their own worth.

The god seen in the likeness of man, is also believed to exhibit the tendencies of man; anger, wrath, biases, judgement, and vengeance; but mostly, being swayable.

The fact is, what you see as your description of God, can get you no more than what you believe can be accomplished by these things without the title.  For, if you see God this way, it is because you know of nothing greater than this, to save you.

Therefore, to know life and possibilities is to meet God for yourself; and form your own description and perception of him.


If you are ready, we will now take you directly to God by the only route he left open to knowing him for yourself.  This is at the line of the Beginning.

Once again, we want you to travel in your consciousness, back to the opposite side of creation. When we step over to pre-beginning, we see absolutely nothing. This is because God is mind; he is not matter, and there is nothing to see. Eyes are sensors, and were not created yet, *because* there was nothing *to* physically sense. All things are experienced in the imagination.

But when we step over onto this side, we sense God in our spirit. We sense the oneness, the belonging, the love. This is spirit; it is total energy and absolute love. The only encounter is sensed in feelings and emotions.

Since you are on the opposite side of creation now, you have not been created, and are also total energy stepping into energy. You too, are spirit.

Spirit is force, it is like the wind or electricity; exuding power, though it is unseen. So, you, stepping over to God, is as a glass of water being poured into the sea. There is no distinguishability.

Here you are now, in this sea of indistinguishable energy. No one, not even you, can see or imagine, any difference between you and God, which is all there is. There is but one thought that you hear and recognize, and that one thought is yours. There is only one will that you recognize, and that is your will.

You are enjoined to the One, now. The field is one, yet it is nothing, and still it is everything. How can this be? Well, since there is nothing to see, this makes it nothing.

However, there is energy, which means that there is something there, unseen, and indistinguishable, and because you are a part of it, you know that it exists. And because it is one, it is everything.

Before we move on, we want you to take a few more seconds in this place where you are now, to take note of this reality. You are one with, and indistinguishable from all the power there is, and all the knowledge there is. And from your awareness, the only thought moving through this place is your thought. The only will is your will. The only desires are yours. And you do not feel foreign, or like an alien. At this point, all things are one.

Now, chew on this thought for a moment: If God is the only one on this side of the beginning and He fills all, then how is there room for you, and how is it that you are accepted as one with the Whole in this place?

If you are a created being, how is it that you are allowed access on this side of the beginning?

Now that we have got your attention, let us dig a little deeper into this thing.

In this part of the scriptures, God is called, or described as Elohiym. The *"ym"* suffix on Elohiym makes it the plural form of Elohi (Lord). Scripture is referring to God as many gods.

This may sound a little off kilter to us because of our teaching that God is one. Even Isaiah 45:5 says, *"I AM the Lord and there is no one else. There is no God beside me."* Nevertheless, scripture is informing us that one God is made up of many gods.

In some places in the Bible they are called Sons of God, and other places they are called Saints in Light. We even give them names, Adonai, El Shaddai, Jehovah Rapha, Jehovah Jireh, Jehovah Nissi, etc. These are not just other names for God. These names are describing the personalities of God. Jehovah Jireh is the god who provides. Jehovah Rapha is the god who heals. And Jehovah Nissi is our Banner.

Each god represents a different thing of importance. Therefore, God is one god made up of many different personalities. Scripture calls it, "One body of many members; with no two members holding the same office." (1Corinthians, Chapter 12).

It is no different than the other religions we criticize for having multiple gods. Our problem is that we do not know enough about the other religions to know that they consider Him one God also, of many personalities.

So, we will understand then, that the God we are seeking, is one God of many different personalities.

Now, the important thing to understand is that He is not the god *with* many different personalities, He is the god who is made up *of* many different personalities. *"For the body is not one member, but many."* 1Corinthians 12:14 KJV. And each of these personalities are gods themselves (Lords), according to the definition of Elohiym.

Now, if it takes all these Lords to make up the one God, then we might understand him better if we compared him to a loaf of bread. Bread is made up of flour, yeast, salt, butter, sugar, milk, and of course, water. All these ingredients mixed together and baked, becomes bread. Before this, there is no such thing as bread. It is not one natural thing, but the outcome of a combination of ingredients.

Before going into the mixing bowl, all these ingredients were stand-alone entities (like gods), having their very own unique taste and texture. Each could have been used for dozens of things which does not include bread. But once they are mixed and baked, they lose their identity to a new creation called bread, which cannot be undone.

In bread, neither ingredient is distinguishable from the other. No matter where you pinch a piece from, to taste, it all tastes like bread. You cannot taste the individuality of any of the ingredients in it; it all tastes the same, and it all looks the same.

So, even though they have lost their identity, they are not lost themselves. They still possess all the power they have always had, except that now, they are sold out to upholding the taste and texture of bread.

If it were possible for one to leave this melding, then bread would no longer be bread. If more sugar is added, then the mixture would become cake. If the yeast were to leave, the outcome would be crackers. This is only to show the power of the individual ingredient.

Now, the coming together of these ingredients was not around one central point or being. They were a voluntary equal. There is no ruling ingredient in bread. There is no Lord over the ingredients; it is just bread.

They are together, one. There is no difference with the personalities of God. Each of these personalities are a power source within themselves, which is like no other. There are no two personalities alike. But their being mixed together makes them, Almighty God. Almighty means, "the might of all." There is none left out. God is he, who is created from the might of all the gods as one. Just as there is no ruling ingredient in bread, there is no ruling god in Elohiym. Though they are a multitude of personalities, they are One.

Unlike bread which became a new creation after the ingredients came together, we would like to think that Elohiym is naturally, every personality. This means that if there was only Elohiym, then he is One, and there would be no need for a ruler.

Since there was only God, we can say that God is not a king, God is not a judge, and God is not a moral lawgiver.  In the case of his oneness, he could only love himself, and therefore, He is absolute love.

Now, since all the personalities were one god, and indistinguishable, then God is everywhere; this makes him omnipresent.  And since all the energies of every personality made up the one God, he is all power, therefore, we call him omnipotent.  Finally, because all the individual knowledge of all the personalities are merged into one, he has all knowledge, and is therefore, omniscient.

So, who is God?  He is everything, in every place, with all power, and all knowledge.  He is Omniscient, Omnipotent, and Omnipresent.

Now, let us see if we can get a description of this invisible God.

We have determined that God is spirit.  He is force.  He is energy.  He is all intelligence, and he is everywhere. And because he has all knowledge, we can say that he is awareness, and he thinks.  But without a body, we can only describe him as mind; consciousness; totally mental. God is Mentality (with a capital "M"). He is not just a type of mentality; he is fully mind.  Mind has all power.  All knowledge is in Mind.  Mind is everywhere. And all creation comes from Mind.

Since this term is less religious, and more scientific, it may help us get a better grip on what was there before creation.

It was this one existence that was all there was. It was this profound depth of consciousness. He was made up of many gods, which were all powerful beings. Each of these beings knew who they were intellectually, but in the whole they were indistinguishable.

They, like salt in bread, was one with the whole, and could not tell where he starts, or where he ends. His only awareness of self was that he existed. And since there was only one power, one thought, and one existence, each personality of the Godhead could legally consider himself the head of the body.

Now, let us go into this body. As we step over from the line of demarcation, we step over into nothingness by visibility. There was nothing to see. There was only an awareness. We cannot say that it was clear because this would be an indication that there was also something cloudy or murky there to compare it to. He was both clear and cloudy. The two cancels each other out, leaving an indescribable nothingness.

But He was there, spirit, consciousness, mind. It was the field of energy that could be recognized as a presence, but not a thing.

Let us take our consciousness to this level of vibration now, (for just a few minutes), and try to sense this presence. A field of gentle accepting energy around us, through us, and losing us in it, as one with it. A feeling of being loved, above and beyond anything we have ever experienced.

It is not staticky, or even attention seeking, but accepting you as one who has moved into the rightful place where you belong.

The only awareness that you should have right now is that you exist in this wonderful fullness. You are existence. You know there is a presence around you, and you feel it in you. You are in this presence, but you do not know whether this presence is just a feeling, or is it you? But because it is mental, it could be anything you want it to be.

It could be your feelings of inner vibration, or the feelings of something around you. It could be a white bright light, or it could be total darkness. It could be eerie, or it could be soothing and encompassing. It could be harsh or loving. It could be hot or cold. Whatever it is, you must realize that at this moment, you are the only awareness that you know of, and the only one being affected by this presence. Any and every decision you could make right now would be 100% of you, and on you.

Whatever you think it is, is exactly what it is to you, of you, and as you. This would be your perception of the All. This is God. There is nothing wrong, neither is there anything right; it is simply your personal perception of what is.

If through this exercise you have sensed God, then you have a description of him.  (John 14:9)

Let us move on to the next phase of perception.

# WHY GOD CREATED

God, being everything, was complete, without any normal needs as we could understand.  Yet we must understand that he had to have a need if he created.

As we know, vanity is an abomination to God.  Therefore, we can be sure that creation was not just a random thing.  Creation was by purpose, and every purpose is driven by a need.  This means that God had a need.  Let us examine this need.

God, like bread, was a makeup of every personality, or every god.  He was Almighty.  He was one.  All the power there is, was one power.  All the thought there was, was one thought.  And He, being one, was in fact, everywhere.

Now, imagine yourself in this position.

Being Omnipresent meant that there was no place that you did not fill.  You would have no place to move because every place is already filled with you.  You are everywhere.  You are the place; with no place to go.

Being Omnipotent means that you have all the power there is, but you cannot use it to move anything. Every part of you is already everywhere, and every part have all power, and could move itself; if it had someplace it could move to.

And as one who is Omniscient, and knowing everything, you would have no one to share this knowledge with. Neither would you have anyone to express yourself to, since all thought is one; and every part of you already knows, because it is, he, who is expressing.

By all intelligent standards, this would constitute having a need.

You would be complete in all your other needs, but your desires would go lacking. There would be an absence of life.

Understand that, just because the ingredients in bread lost its identity to the whole, it did not lose its knowledge or awareness of itself. Outside of the whole each is an individual, capable of doing a multitude of things that does not include bread.

In this same manner, all the individual personalities of God, while losing their identity in the Godhead, cannot forget who they are as an individual.

Though Elohiym was totally complete in his love, there was still one thing missing.

That one thing was life. Many of us think of life as simply existing. It is not. Existence has been used as the noun for life, but life is really a verb. It is vitality. Vitality is animation; it is liveliness. Vitality is movement, interacting, having spark, effervescence, push, or drive. Life is expressing oneself and experiencing that expression.

God was everything, but not one part of him was able to express itself, or to experience itself while in the whole, because all the power of self was being used to uphold the fullness of the Godhead.

Therefore, God *did* have a need, an uncharted need.

So, we *can* say that God had a need, and that need was to experience himself in the magnificence of all the personalities that he is, individually. God created because he wanted to experience life. He wanted to express himself in every way he desired, and to experience every expression.

The Almighty created because every personality in him longed for the opportunity to express himself/herself as an individual; and to experience the reality of those expressions.

The only purpose of creation is for God to express himself as an individual, and to experience what it is like to operate as himself, outside of the whole. This was His good pleasure, and this was what he deemed life.

# HOW GOD CREATED

God was all there was, and all his power was being used to uphold the fullness of the Almighty. As we have come to understand about bread; if any ingredient were moved out of its place, bread would no longer be bread. So with God. To maintain the perfect balance of the Almighty would take the fullness of dedication of each individual god as one.

Understand that God is 100% energy; and that energy is consciousness; it is mind. To remove the mind from anything it has formed, would be to lose the formation. Since Elohiym has always been the Almighty, it is literally impossible for him to become something else, or to turn his full attention to something else. So, in order to express himself as the individual he wanted to experience, he had to create a proxy.

Since God was mind, the only way he could create was in imagination. Thus, he said, *"Let us make man in our imagination, after our likeness; and let them have dominion over all creation."*

Now, in John 17:5, Jesus said in prayer, *"Father glorify thou me with thine own self; with the glory I had with thee before the world was."* We will have to factor in here, that there was something or someone else with Elohiym before the world was.

We know that it was not a direct part, or character of the original Godhead. All of this was One. Jesus used the term, "With thee", meaning an associate; not of the original. There was someone else with Elohiym before the world was formed.

In John 1:14, where John was referring to the Word being made flesh to dwell among men, he added, *"And we beheld his glory, as of the only Begotten of the Father."*

This was the only Begotten Son. The proxy of God was his own son; made in His image and likeness. Hebrews 1:3 says that he was the express image of his person. This "being" was everything in exact form and makeup that God was. This was the mirror image of Elohiym.

Colossians 2:9 says, *"In him was the fullness of the Godhead, bodily."* This meant that a replica in exact form was made of every personality in the Son also, as it was in the Father.

Therefore, the "Man" that Elohiym imagined as himself, was his son, the Christ. "Himself" was the only image that he knew to emulate because there was only him known. Colossians 1:15 says, *"Who is the image of the invisible God, the first born of every creature."*

This man that God created to express himself through, was his only Begotten Son, his proxy. This was not Jesus. Jesus did not come on the scene until 2000 years ago. He came as the *image* of the first man, the Christ. Therefore, he called himself, "The Son of Man". Matthew 16:13 says, *"When Jesus came into the coasts of Caesarea Philippi, he asked his disciples saying, Whom do men say that I the son of man am?"*

Christ, as the first man, was the life that Elohiym would express himself through. He was the expression of God, and everything God wanted to experience was in him.

John 1:1-4 says, *"In the beginning was the Word: The Word was with God, and the Word was God. The same was in the beginning with God. All things were made by him, and without him was nothing made that was made. In him was life, and the life was the light of men."* Since God, being all that is, could not move to express himself, he could only express himself through words, which in the spirit realm is thought. A "Word" is an expression, and therefore, the proxy of God, who was his son, who was his expression, which was his word. Everything was summed up in the Christ, the Son of God.

The Bible begins with the words, *"In the beginning God created..."*

Now, since the Christ was the first, of all creation, he was the "Beginning". He was not in the beginning, or at the beginning; this man, the Christ, is the "Beginning". The rise of all life. (Colossians 1:15-19)

Therefore, the Bible says "IN" the beginning, and not at the beginning, God created. All things were created in IN him. He was the proxy of Elohiym, and God was going to express and experience himself through this surrogate. And therefore, everything was in him; the Christ, who was the proxy of God.

This is why the Bible constantly emphasizes, "IN Christ". Our lives, our blessings, our salvation; all of it, is IN Christ. "In Him we live and move and have our being. (Acts 17:28) He is the only way to God. (John 14:6)

Now, therefore, not to lose place, we will end our explanation of the proxy, and continue with the "How" of creation.

In the Beginning, God created the heaven and the earth. The heaven and the earth are together, the whole of the universe, which was not created in an outside atmosphere or environment from God. There is not an outside to God. This wholeness of all that exist was made in Christ, the "Beginning". All life is in Christ. (Colossians 1:19) And Christ is in God. Christ is God's imagination of himself.

# The Creation of the Universe

The universe is not a place randomly thrown together as many may think. Every place, and everything in this universe was meticulously thought about, and created to perfection.

Every personality in Elohiym was of a different mind, but together as the Almighty, they are One. This alliance formed the greatest engineering mind that could ever be imagined. This Mind created the universe. Nothing was missed, omitted, or eliminated. This was the first perfection.

Understand that the universe was not made, simply, this beautiful place to reside in, but it was engineered as an instrument. The word, instrument, comes from the word *instruct-ment*. To instruct means to construct or implement; that is, to show. The term *"ment"*, comes from mental, the mind. Together they mean, *"To show the mind."* An instrument is used to show the mind.

Take for instance, a saxophone, a musical instrument. This piece of equipment is created to show the world what is in the mind of the musician. When he/she blows into it, this is not just a random breath, but an expression of their emotions, who they are being.

A sad person would probably play the blues, while a cool, laid-back person would probably express himself with a little smooth jazz. And perhaps a well-balanced and centered person would play something classical. Even an angry person can express himself through this instrument.

There is no difference in the universe. Because Elohiym wanted to express himself as all that he is in each individual personality, and to experience each of these expressions, he created this flawless instrument that is incapable of failing. It was created to give him the precise experience to every expression he made.

 Suppose you wanted to express a high note on the saxophone, then a low note, and a return to the high note again. This instrument was created with keys to depress, which will help you to experience exactly what you want to hear, when you learn which keys to depress. Likewise, the universe, as well, was created to give you whatever you desire to experience once you learn how to express it.

Have you ever yelled hello in a canyon, or a cave? This was the expression you put out; and the experience was returned to you in the form of an echo. If hello did not return to you as bonsoir, then you received the perfect experience to your expression.

This is what the universe was created for. It is absolutely impossible for anyone to prevent another person from expressing themselves. And it is also impossible for one to express himself without receiving the perfectly matched experience of reality for his expression. This is an eternal law that is a part of the makeup of the universe, called the Law of Cause and Effect. *"Be not deceived, God is not mocked: for whatsoever a man soweth, that shall he also reap."* (Galatians 6:7)

Genesis 2:1 says, *"Thus the heavens and the earth were finished, and all the host of them."* Since there was no such thing as physical material, the creation of the universe was the forming of thought in God. This majestic instrument was created in the imagination of God. Imagination is all that existed. He saw it completely, in the only way he could, and <u>liked</u> it. Therefore, the creation of it was finished.

Now, Jesus said, in Matthew 5:28, *"But I say unto you, that whosoever looketh on a woman to lust after her hath committed adultery with her already in his heart."* Now, this statement had nothing to do with adultery or being condemned, it was simply an analogy. What was being said here was the fact that a completed thought (Faith) is the substance of the thing hoped for. This is a complete visualization of the desire. The emotions, or reaction, caused by this completed thought is the evidence of the existence of the thing not yet seen in the physical.

If you get an emotion from a thing thought about, or if it causes you to act or react, then this thing already exists in its fullness. It does not need physical representation to do what it has already done in its invisible state.

God's reaction to what he created was to like it. He called it "good".

So, in order to complete the plans of creation, He delivered this universe to a host. A host is the carrier. This is the person, in whose house, the party is being thrown. It is the hotel where the V.I.P. is staying. It is the arena where the boxing match is being held. The host is the person who is the carrier of the virus, or the demon spirit. It is the dog on whom the fleas have made their home.

Scripture says that the universe was finished, and all the host of this universe. This means that it was not put outside of us as we may believe when we look around us. And we are not put into it. It is, in fact, put inside of us. The Christ, the son of Elohiym, who was created for God to express and experience his good pleasure through, was the host of the universe.

The first man, Christ, was the exact makeup of Elohiym. He was the makeup of every spirit personality. He was the Bread of Life. This means that all life was equally one in him. He was not one over all; he was one as all, or all as one. Since every man's life is in Christ as the Christ, then every living being is a carrier of the universe.  It is in us as mind, and not outside of us as some material olio.

So, we can say that the instrument that is created to give us an experience to our every expression cannot fail us, because it is built into us.  What we see on the outside is only an outer sensing (the experience) of what is in us.

Have you ever played with a virtual reality game?  It is only a visor put over your eyes, but when you turn it on, you experience an entirely different world from where you are.  It is so very realistic, that it takes your emotions to practically every level.  The only difference between this and the universe is that the universe operates by your thoughts and emotions.  It is mind connect.  Thus, the universal law, "As within, so without.  As without so within.  As above, so below.  As below, so above."

# INSIDE THE DREAM

Now, since God is eternal, and the universe was created for his good pleasure, then the universe had to be created for eternal use.

Because the universe is imagination, it is thus temporal, and is apt to eventually fade away. For this reason, God created it by laws. For instance, everything that was created from the dust (energy field) will return to the energy field for refreshing.

Every tree and plant will produce seeds that will reproduce after its own kind.

Every animal and insect will reproduce after its own kind.

New gases will be formed from the waste or use of other things to replace the gases used to glow our sun and other stars.

Oxygen will be the intake for humans to live. Humans will inhale this oxygen and exhale carbon dioxide, which is the intake for plants for their life. The output of plants taking in the carbon dioxide would be oxygen, which replaces that which was consumed by humans.

The cells that makes up the tissues forming the human body are replaced many times throughout the human lifetime to keep it formed according to the force of the imagination. In fact, according to science, cell replacement is so rapid that there is, in all actuality, no human body over seven years old. Literally every cell in the body has been replaced many times.

There are laws that keep creation in existence, and there are laws to the way creation operates. For instance, the earth makes a full rotation around the sun every 365.25 days, while the moon is rotating around the earth every 28 days. The earth itself, makes a full rotation every 24 hours while spinning at 1000 miles per hour at the center. If either would decrease or increase in speed, it could possibly slip off its axis and perhaps collide with another body moving in the same solar system.

But because it has no life of its own, it cannot move of its own accord, and is eternally safe in the imagination of God.

Every quarter rotation of the moon around the earth has a lunar effect on the planet. Every quarter rotation around the sun has a seasonal change on the plants, seeds, and the inhabitants of the planet.

There is a season to sow, and a season to reap. There is a season for summer, and a season for winter. The sun causes water vapors to rise from the seas to form clouds in the heavens, and the clouds carries the water to needed places to release it for nurturing and refreshing.

All this works by laws that are permanently set in creation to keep it operating in a consistent and orderly manner to sustain and serve the inhabitants. These are not the only laws, but there are laws that governs absolutely everything and every operation in the universe. These laws are permanent, absolute, and therefore, dependable. Water will never boil until the temperature reaches 212 degrees Fahrenheit, and it will never freeze until the temperature drops to 32 degrees Fahrenheit. Gravity will always pull everything to the ground that is not of the air's atmosphere, and one plus one will always equal two.

The universe is a self-sufficient, self-repairing, self-regenerating, living entity that God created as an instrument to give him any, and everything he wanted to experience as an inhabitant of this Time and Space Continuum. The universe was for his good pleasure; not for someone else, because no one else existed or exists. All things are of him, is him, and is made as him, for his good pleasure. Why would He create it for his misery?

A good thing to remember is that **THE UNIVERSE WILL NEVER FAIL YOU.** It is watching you.

You might consider the universe in the manner of the old global surveillance conspiracy, "Big Brother is Watching

You". The universe is literally watching you, and giving attention to everything you think, say, and do. For it will answer you.

Not in a scary, conspiring sort of way; but for the express purpose of knowing your every expression, that it may answer you with an exact return of experience to all you express. It has no other purpose. It was engineered especially for this. For God's good pleasure.

**Note:** The boy who cried wolf, really did summon the wolf. (Fairytale)

# How the Universe Works

*Learning How to Manipulate Creation*

Genesis 1:1-4, *"In the beginning God created the heaven and the earth. And the earth was without form and void: and darkness was upon the face of the deep. And the Spirit of God moved upon the face of the waters. And God said, let there be light: and there was light. And God saw the light, that it was good: and God divided the light from the darkness."*

The most powerful and perfect instrument created was the universe. It was created to serve the dream of God's imagination. It was created not to provide "things", but to automatically provide experiences to every expression. "Things" come to uphold the experience of the expression. Let us say a person expresses anger. The universe is programmed to automatically bring things into this person's life that will continuously cause him to get, or be, angry: a flat tire, a speeding ticket, etc. As long as he expresses anger, the universe will answer him with causes to provoke anger. He will continue to be served by anger until he changes his expression.

Please understand that this is not a punishment. This is a service. And a change of expression is the only thing that can interrupt this service.

Ecclesiastes 5:9 says, *Moreover, the profit of the earth is for all: the king himself is served by the field."*

When God created the universe, it was from his imagination. His imagination was this field of energy that filled the Son. This was all the energy dedicated to creation. The field of energy that filled the Son was no different than the energy that Elohiym himself was. Scientists have measured this existence and calls them Dark Matter (creation), and Dark Energy (God).

The definition of matter is "Significance of mind." The *imagination* of Dark Energy became Dark Matter. (i.e. unknown energy and unknown matter.)

Sensed matter and dark matter are of the same field. This is, therefore, an indication that dark matter is the Field of Creation established by Elohiym.

Scripture says that it was without form, and void; and darkness was upon the face of the deep. The word "face" was used here to help us understand that it was the forefront of this field. It is as the frontal cortex, or control center of our brain, which helps us to form, or make sense of our emotions. Formlessness and darkness are saying that It had no shape, and no recognizable contents; it was unable to be understood, and therefore nothing.

The sense of nothingness was its purpose. To be un-recognizable left the inhabitants of creation without something to sense. This would cause his attention to be led by what is sensed. It was created this way so that nothing would be responsible for the life that man experiences, but the expressions he freely puts out.

Now, understand that the creation of heaven and earth was this field of total energy; just as Elohiym was total energy. Energy has no shape of its own but can be shaped by harnessing and forming.

250,000 volts of electrical energy passing through the main line on your street, can be shifted off to a home requiring a max of 240 volts and perhaps 150 amps to run on. Without being harnessed, 250,000 volts would burn up every light and appliance in the home. But, because this energy can be harnessed, a simple circuit breaker can stand before this massive power and channel it down to lighting a 120-volt lamp without any damage whatsoever. A breaker box with varying breakers could harness this power and channel this power to appliances requiring 120 and 240 volts of electricity, at the same time.

So, energy is controllable; and if man's life is all energy, then man must learn to control it himself; or, *accept the fact that it will be controlled by someone else as long as he exists.*

The harnessing of energy in creation's Field of Energy is through imagination. Imagination is the form shaped by the force of thoughts. For those who smoke, or once smoked, remember the circles of smoke you enjoyed making through a puff of wind. It was the forced of the energy from the wind that shaped the smoke into its donut image.

Your breath of wind was invisible, but it was energy; and the power of that invisible energy shaped the smoke into your desired formation. A believed thought is energy, and it harnesses the energy of the field, and brings it into the shape of the imagination. Just as a circuit breaker can stand before 250,000 volts of electricity and harness it down to light a lamp limited to 120 volts, a thought can go into this massive Field of Creation and create a desired experience; no matter how large or how small it may be.

God showed us in the second and third verse of Genesis, chapter 1, of the Bible, how to manipulate the power of this field to get whatever you desire. In fact, it is not manipulating the field, but rather, using the field the way it was designed to be used.

Let us examine this. The second verse says, "The earth was without form and void: and darkness was upon the face of the deep: and the Spirit of God moved upon the face of the waters. The optimal statement here is, "The Spirit of God moved upon..." The universe was this massive field of unseen, unfelt, indistinguishable energy

(Like water).   The Spirit of God, which was his "emotions", was expressed in this field.  The spirit of a thing is its emotion.   The spirit of the party is in the emotions of the goers.  The spirit of a church is expressed by the emotions of the leader and the congregation. Spirit is simply emotions, and emotion is the only force that expresses.  Whether we know it or not, all our goals or desires in life is to obtain one result.  That one result is the emotion associated with having, being, or doing.

The Spirit of God moved "upon" this existence.  The words, "moved upon" does not mean to hover over as we have been taught concerning this verse. To *move upon* something is to affect it.  When a disease *moves upon* a person, it affects them with sickness.  When assailants *move upon* a victim, he is usually injured or killed.  Even when joy *moves upon* a person, they are affected with happiness and peace.  "Move upon" means to affect.

When God said, "Let there be light", it was his emotion affecting this energy, thus harnessing it, forming it, and bringing it into experience.  The Bible said, "And there was light".

Scripture shows us this because God wants us to know that words alone are not effective.  Though they were meant to create, words have no power, alone.  Hebrews 1:3 is saying that the Christ was the brightness of God's glory, and the express image of his person.  But it also said that he was upholding all things by the word of his power, not the power of his word.  Words do not have power, but they transport power. The power that words transport is emotion. Emotions carried about by words is the unstoppable force that is guaranteed to get you an exact experience to anything you express.

Jesus said in Matthew 18:19, "*Again I say unto you, if two of you shall agree on earth, as touching anything they shall ask, it shall be done for them of my Father which is in heaven.*" While the two of you could possibly mean two people in perfect agreement, here, the *two of you* on earth is really meaning your emotions and your thoughts. This is you. When your emotions come into alignment with your thoughts, nothing can stop this creation from coming into your experience. This is how the universe was created to work; and it never fails.

Your emotion is the force that you, as spiritual energy, is exuding. This force shapes the creative energy, of which you are, just as our breath of wind shapes the smoke into circles; and *you* will be changed by this reshaping. As we said earlier, a creation is completed when it brings an emotion, or a reaction.

Hebrews 11:1 says, "*Now faith is the substance of things hoped for, the evidence of things not seen.*" In other words, our thoughts with emotions reveals our belief, and belief is the substance of the thing created. What we believe is our reality. And reaction is the evidence of the completion of the thing not seen.

No matter how you look at it, God created the universe so that emotions, which is your most perfect expression, is the power of creation in this field. The force of this picture in your mind, when completed with emotion, will shape the energy of this field into the exact experience that is being expressed.

This means that you are the only one with the power to shape your life; no matter how much you pray, beg, or try to convince an outside God. Only you can shape your life. This power has been released to you, and you alone. Elohiym will not come in to change the power that is yours, as an individual Lord, to control. Genesis 1:28 says, *"And God blessed them, and God said unto them, Be fruitful, and multiply, and replenish the earth, and subdue it: and have dominion over the fish of the sea, and of the fowl of the air, and over every living thing that moveth upon the earth."* This is God's word, and it cannot be changed.

Of God's work, it is completed. Of Jesus' work, it is finished. The responsibility for your life is now, and irrevocably, yours.

There is one other thing we should know about this passage in Genesis 1:1-4. In the 4th verse it says, *"And God saw the light that it was good; and God divided the light from the darkness."* The Field of Energy was totally invisible. There was no way to describe it. Darkness was its cover. But when God called the light, he divided the light from the darkness. Where did the darkness come from? Darkness is describable.

Well, the fact is that there is a law built into the universe called the Law of Polarity, also known as the Law of Duality. For everything that is created, there is an opposite. There is nothing that can be described without being compared to its opposite. No one can be tall, unless he is being compared to someone who is short. Nothing can be sweet unless it is being compared to something bitter. Without an opposite, nothing has a description.

These two, light and darkness, obviously have different, or opposite, effects. Paul says, in Romans 7:21, *I find then a law, that when I would do good evil is present with me."* He obviously did not attempt to create the evil; but it showed up.

God saw the light that it was good. This means that darkness was not the good in this case, and it was not needed now except for comparison. So, he divided them to the extreme, to different poles. To the extremity of back to back. Nothing is ever so close, and yet so far away.

Now even though they are separated to extremes, they must show up together for defining purposes. This means that whatever you create, the opposite will always show up with it, but they are always facing opposite directions. Though they show up together, they are on different planes. Each is going in the opposite direction from the other. What coin shows up with a head and not a tail?

As God did with the light, it is up to you to define and separate. He saw the light, defined it as good, then divided it from the darkness. He chose the light.

The danger of this is that when you see the two of them show up together, you may fear reaching for the good while it seems attached to the bad. The good news is that you have the authority to choose and separate.

Many people have chosen the wrong pole because of their belief that they are not worthy of having what they desire. And perhaps more, being led by their ego to be right about their judgement. But there is another law built into creation called, "The Law of Perpetual Transmutation of Energy". This law assures us that all energy is in motion, and all energy that is in motion will eventually appear as matter or in a physical form. This means that a higher vibration of energy of the opposite of that which you are experiencing, will cause a transmutation in your experience.

Should you begin to believe more on the opposite side of your experience, you raise the vibration of it. This will cause that side to begin to appear. Because they are opposites, as one appears the other will disappear. Think a certain way about a thing, and the opposite way will disappear from your life experiencing.

# Understanding Man in the Dream

Remember, Elohiym is the dreamer.  His son, made in his image and likeness, is his surrogate.  He is the first man, the Christ, in whom the Father will experience His dreams through.

This first man, being in the image of Elohiym, was made up of an exact copy of every god personality that his Father was.  He was not the host of these gods; these gods together were the makeup of the son.

These god personalities called Elohiym, were all dedicated to the work of upholding the Godhead.  However, as the son, while they were still one, they were yet free to think individually.  They were created with no other responsibilities, but to express themselves as individuals, and to sense the experience of those expressions.

`Each personality, as this first man, began to live by imagining himself or herself as the being that they felt they were.  The power from the force of their imaginations entered the Field of Creation, which was in them, and formed the exact image of how they saw themselves. These characters became living souls. And so, began the dream.

Every created being was different, because every personality, being different, had a different view of who he/she was. *"So God created man in his own image, in the imagination of God created he him; male and female created he them."* Genesis 1:27. This image was the god personality's imagination of himself.

So, God personally lives his life through, and as, this man whom He formed in the Field of Creation through his imagination. This man is literally God in his earthly form.

Now, since this image called man was the god personality's imagination of himself, and since the earth was created for God's good pleasure, there is no way that either of these can ever go away. The earth and the man are mind-made, and the way God sees things. He has made these for his own life, He cannot change, and *these* will therefore, never go away.

Let us break this down a little further. The universe is God's created instrument, used to give him the experience of life, by answering every expression. Since this is the only instrument, with none other to compare it to or to rival it, we would have to agree that it is perfect. It is in the mind of God as the means to experience his life. And as long as God is the living God, it cannot go away. Where will it go to? Can God forget?

It is therefore permanent in the mind of God, which is all there is. Where else can it go?

The man, who is God's imagination of himself, is the only way Elohiym can express and experience what he desires to experience as life. Without man, He cannot enter the dream. And without activity in the dream, there is no life. Each soul, or man, is God's permanent view of who he is. Man is not a puppet, nor is he an impersonal toy; man is God in person. Therefore, man is eternal.

The body (image) of man formed in the Creation Field may expire and change to meet the new expressions of self, but the soul (mind/consciousness) is the permanent ongoing man who is the Lord God himself. The expiring and changing of bodily forms are only for the expression of new growth. This is what we call reincarnation, or the Bible term, "Resurrection". (If the soul does not die, then what is needed to be resurrected but the flesh, which is expired. As God lives, the soul will live as God's view of himself. Eternally, world without end.

Now, man's role in the dream is not as chaotic as it has been made to seem. The dream is the Lord's constant imaging of himself in life, and man's role is simple. Hebrews 10:16 says, *"This is the covenant that I will make with them after those days, saith the Lord, I will put my laws in their hearts, and in their mind will I write them."* While the word used here is "laws", it is actually interpreted as "desires". The Lord is saying that the full role of man in creation, is to do the desires of his heart, and that which is inspired in his mind. The Greek word for this is "*Charis*"; interpreted as "Grace". Grace is defined as, divine inspiration, influence in the heart. That is it! The man simply needs to be in touched with himself as Lord God, and to do the desires of his heart. That is his only purpose. Everything else is man's idea of honoring or giving back to God. While this may seem noble, it is not obedience. Scripture tells us that disobedience is as witchcraft.

# Elohiym's Work is Finished

The difference between Elohiym and Christ, the son, is that Elohiym is one. He knows as one, thinks as one, is the power of one, and he is indistinguishably one. He cannot act as an individual god personality. The son, however, is one also, but with the freedom to think as each of the different gods or personalities that he is, individually. So, Elohiym created his son, the proxy or surrogate, in whom He will express and experience his life through.

Since he was going to live through this proxy, God put everything that pertains to life in the Son. This everything included his desires, and the universe which was created to give him every desire that he expressed. This was it: six days of work.

Genesis 2:1-3 says, *"Thus the heavens and the earth were finished, and <u>all</u> the host of them. And on the seventh day God ended his work which he had made; and he rested on the seventh day from <u>all</u> his work which he had made. And God blessed the seventh day and sanctified it: because that in it he rested from <u>all</u> his work which God created and made."*

Each of the gods as Elohiym, simultaneously (in the unison of one), created a man in the imagination of who he saw himself as being, as either male or female. ("Let *us* make man in *our* imagination, after *our* likeness".) This man was the son of God, birth from his mind. Each of these entities, being one as the Christ, was the host of the universe. The only way they could see and utilize the universe is as it was created in them as mind.

The will of God was in their hearts and mind, and they were each, the individual personalities of God. He put his desires in their hearts and mind that they would always love and think about the things that God wanted to express and experience as them.

Life is God's dream, and he is living it as man. The dream consists of every possible scenario that we have experienced up to today, plus an eternity more. Elohiym created every possible way to experience all things desired, through the expression of the host. Since God is All, then all life is God, and there is therefore, no impossibilities in life.

While all things may not be expedient, all things are lawful to experience as the God who is all.

Now, as scripture says, after six days, all the work of God was finished. And He rested on the seventh day, because all his work was finished. Elohiym retired from Creator to become the Watcher of what he had created. To sit back and enjoy himself in the act of living.

Were there any special, or ordered ways He wanted life to be had? No! Life is simply expressing one's self and experiencing those expressions. There was nothing special to do to satisfy God, but to honestly live out your heart felt expressions and accept the experience that it brings.

After pointing out that God had finished all these preparations to go into his rest, the third verse uniquely points out that it was Elohiym who had finished the work. It specifically pointed this out to let us know that all this work was done by the one mind of the Whole: or the "Wholly One" (Holy One). From this point, everything else would be done by the individual personalities from their own individual bodies. The Lord Gods.

Elohiym had prepared everything and left the door opened for man to enter His rest and take advantage of building his life through the powerful force of imagination.

Now, in the fourth verse, we see a change in character. It is no longer Elohim doing the work; his work is finished. It is the Lord God in control now. Elohiym was no Lord because He was one. But, the Lord God, being given all dominion, was the Lord and ruler of his own individual life and world in creation.

The Lord God is the individual personality of God living in creation as the conscious mind, which is man. The mind is made up of two parts, the conscious and the subconscious.  The conscious mind is the objective awareness which is in the dream (the earth); he expresses.  The subconscious mind, which is the subjective provider, is the power of producing the experience in the universe.  He resides deep inside the conscious mind, and will bring to life, every fully thought out expression.

Now, the operation of living is to simply take life as you imagine it for yourself and go into the *"rest"* of Elohiym. The provisions have already been prepared for you in any form you may choose. But you (and only you) must choose through your believable imaginations.

The subconscious mind, being the subjective, is literally Christ in man; he is the Wholly, or Holy Spirit.  He is the Field of Creation.  The universe is in him.  When the conscious mind expresses a curiosity, or a belief, it is taken by the subconscious to be an expression.  Thus, it is the automatic operation of this instrument in him, to deliver a production of experience to match this expression, or rather, to turn this expression into a reality.

A simple way of putting it is that, all Elohiym's work was left in the Field of Creation, which is in everyone; and everyone has dominion over this field in them.  This field is all energy.  When we imagine anything, the force of our imagination forms, in this field, the things thought about.  And it is formed in such a way that it can be experienced just the way they were imagined. There was nothing visible in the field, except that which is created by the imaging of the individual.

So, do we call upon the Father, God; who is Elohiym, the Father of Christ? No! His work is finished.

Do we call upon Jesus? No! His redeeming work is finished also.

 We have no one to call upon but ourselves, as the sons of God. We are the Lord Gods who possess the dominion to lord over our own lives, whether it aligns with the grace of the spirit within, or not. We still make our own choices and are responsible for the way we see ourselves, and this world. There is nothing wrong except that you may not enjoy the experience you are having as a result of your expressions of yourself, and your life, and the world that you live in.

If you do not like the experience that you are getting as your life, then transform yourself by the renewing of your mind. (Romans 12:2)

# GOD'S REST, AND HOW TO ENTER INTO IT

*"There remaineth therefore, a rest to the people of God. For he that is entered into his rest, he also hath ceased from his own works, as God did from his. Let us labour therefore, to enter into that rest, lest any man fall after the same example of unbelief."* Hebrews 4:9-11.

Why was God's rest so important to him? Because all the work he had done and finished, was for His plans and eternal purpose in life.

When God decided that he wanted to become the Living God, He gave freedom to every personality of himself, to have life by expressing and experiencing himself in any way he desired, for eternity. But, because no two were alike, He had to create a universe that would accommodate them all.

So, He took six days to create a universe whose foundation is made of laws that would render unto anyone, the exact experience to the expression he is making a prototype of, with his thoughts, words, and emotions. The universe was designed and built to give anyone, any and everything needed, to have the full experience of his expression. This meant that all life was prepared for man to live by his beliefs. We are believers.

After these six days, the Almighty rested, because everything was created and finished, to do everything it was created to do on earth. His "rest" was in the fact that all the labor was finished. There was no one who would need to labor to have what he desires to have. No experience was limited for man. All the work was finished at the foundation of the earth. In fact, all the work was the foundation of the universe; and man is the host of this universe. He simply needs to believe, and act upon those beliefs. His labor is to become the person fitted to the things he desires to experience.

For this reason, God expected everyone to enter his rest.

This was the problem He had with the Hebrews according to scripture, in the Book of Hebrews. They had prayed for centuries, for God to free them up from slavery in Egypt and bring them into the Promised Land of milk and honey. This was the land of Canaan that God had promised to Abraham, Isaac, and Jacob, for their descendants, forever.

So, God sent Moses to tell them that He heard their prayer, and he had come to set them free. Now, the problem with this is that every one of these Hebrews was born into slavery. They prayed for freedom from slavery, but because they knew nothing else, they were only looking for freedom of the flesh. The only thing they knew in their minds was slavery. So, God had a work of mental transformation to do with them before He would release them from Egypt.

This is a problem with most of the world today. We think that we can move to any lifestyle we desire with our present mind. Yet so few seek to realize and understand that it is the mind we have, that got us where we are.

The Lord had to get these Hebrew slaves to change their minds about who they were; and make this change a habit. This was a spiritual thing.

When He brought plagues upon Egypt by Moses and Aaron, the destruction did not touch the Hebrews. This should have made them feel like special people, deserving of the Promised Land. But God went a little further and made them borrow the riches of the people of Egypt to depart with.

Why did they need riches; there were no Malls in the desert? In fact, with all the riches they departed with, they could not even buy water. However, God's purpose was not for them to spend the riches, his purpose was to give them a rich mind; to wash away the slave mentality.

The mind (spirit) was the important thing here. Their Lord had already prepared a place for them in the Land of Promise, where all the work had already been done. A place where they would obtain lands and houses and cattle, fields, and vineyards that they neither bought, planted, built, or raised. Their only job was to assume the identity of a people who deserved it, to gain access into this rest. To trust God enough to cross this desert, despite "whatever", to come into their land.

But the problem with these people was that they had a slave's mentality. They dreamed of having it but could not see themselves as literally possessing it. As much as they loved God and desired to be in this land of milk and honey and even as much as they believed that it was promised to them, most of them could not make it in.

When Moses first obtained their release and got them out of Egypt and into the desert, they sang and dance for the next couple of days. But the problem was that they were slaves, they had never been out of the gates of the City. After a couple of days of singing and dancing, the burdens of the wilderness began to affect them, and they began to lose their vision of the land of milk and honey, and they began to envision themselves perishing in the desert. They began to complain at every turn.

These people who had walked out of the land of Egypt by the hand of God, as a mighty people, were now seeing themselves as victims of the wilderness.

So, God, in an effort to rebuild their self-confidence, caused Pharaoh to decide to go after them with the intent of cutting them off. The Lord purposely led the Hebrews into a trap, to prove to them that they were worthy. They were between two mountain ranges, with the Red Sea in front of them, and Pharaoh's Army closing in on their rear. God caused the Red Sea to open a roadway for them by the waters parting into two walls, that they may walk through on dry land. Then God drowned Pharaoh's Army as they pursued in the attempt to overtake them.

Once again, they began to sing and dance. However, this did not last very long. Within the next few days, they were complaining about no water and no food. They were accusing Moses of bringing them and their wives and children out of their secure homes, and into the desert to die.

God showed them the impossible, by giving them water from a rock, and food rained down from heaven. But it was not long again that they began to make victims of themselves once more. They could not get rid of that slave's mentality. They claimed to be tired of the bread and wanted meat. God caused quails to fly in that they may have their request of meat.

Then God brings them within reach of the Promised Land, and told them to send in twelve trusted men to spy out the land for its contents, believing that this would surely raise their confidence level to go in.

100% of the twelve men that went in, returned with the report and proof that this indeed, was the land of milk and honey. But because of their self-victimization, and their unbelief, 83% of this dozen also brought an addendum to the report. While they reported that this is surely the Promised Land, they, in spite of all God had brought them through, reported that it was impossible to go into the land because it was infested with giants; and they felt like grasshoppers before them.

This land was the dream; it was the rest that God had promised them. They had no labor before them. They got released from slavery without a fight. They destroyed Pharaoh's Army without lifting a weapon. They crossed a sea without getting wet. A rock gave them water, and the sky even rained down food for them. The work had already been done.

All they had to do was believe, and assume the rights, the position, the thought, and the act that they were the people chosen to go into this land of milk and honey. They were the ones who would get the houses, land, vineyards, fields, and cattle, without having to earn it.

It was theirs. It was in the rest that God had prepared for them. There is an old saying, "Heaven is a prepared place for a prepared people." Likewise, what you get is only what you are prepared for.

However, when they would not believe enough to walk into the rest that God had prepared for them (and remain in that belief), The Almighty decided that they would remain as Nomads in the desert for the next forty years; until all the non-believers would die without entering the Promised Land.

Now, the second chapter of Genesis, in the scriptures, tells us that after six days of labor, God's work was finished; and he rested. God rested because there was nothing left to do. Everything was already prepared for him to experience any life he desires through his avatar, man.

This means that all of creation was about freely having life. No one was created to hustle for this life. Everything was already prepared to have the dream life that everyone desires. The only labor man must tend with, is the labor to stay in the dream. To walk by faith, and not by sight. That is, to endure until he reached the promise. There is an old proverb from scripture, paraphrased this way: "The race does not go to the swift, nor the battle to the strong, but to him that endureth to the end."

Hebrews 4:1 says, *"Let us therefore fear, lest a promise being left us of entering into his rest, any of you should seem to come short of it."*

To enter this rest is to understand that there is no labor you have to produce to live the life that you desire. He has prepared everything. You simply need to imagine being and living the life you desire, and the universe is already made up to render unto you all the things that you believe will bring about the experience of this imagination. He has done the labor, and you are simply entering into the finished work, from which He rest.

The real key to entering God's rest is found in Hebrews 4:7a, "*Again, he limited a certain day, saying in David, Today…*" This passage of scripture is telling us that since we are eternal beings, there is no tomorrow. Today is "NOW". It is literally impossible to become something tomorrow. One hundred years from now, tomorrow still would not have come, but it will still be today and now.

So, you cannot wait, or expect something to be created over a period of time. One must have a definite chief aim and purpose. One must know who he/she is now; and walk in that profession. Even the Bible tells you to stand fast in the profession of your faith. Unless you know how to express being who you desire to be, you can only continue to be who you are being now.

If you desire to live a wealthy life, then you must express having reached that pinnacle already. And no matter how much the world says that you owe them, or the world tries to tell you that you are poor, you must not be moved by them. You must stay at the pinnacle of your desire now, today, and always. This is faith.

You may not have all that you desire immediately, because you have never actually been there to know how to express it, but you will have exactly as much as you believe and express.  No amount of full belief will be left unexperienced.  And if you standfast in the belief that you are who you desire to be, scripture says you will be transformed from glory to glory to glory.

Understand that when you have got clothes on your body, food on your table, and a roof over your head, you have everything you need.  But when you let someone make you believe you are poor, despite having everything you need, then you are indeed poor.  And the only thing you can "rest" in, is poverty.

Now, if you decide to maintain the obvious fact that you have everything you need, then, when your emotions align with your thoughts, words, and actions, you will have entered the rest of God.  And by law, the universe must equal your beliefs with all the things that would give you the emotions of the wealthy being of your immediate belief.

# YOU MUST HAVE AN UNDERSTANDING OF MIND

I believe that the biggest problem with life in this world is that the average person does not understand the mind. We believe that we have a mind, located somewhere in our brains.  Some even think that mind is just a temporary thought.  But this takes us far off course of understanding what it is, where it is, and how to use it.

Think about this:  There is hardly a person on this earth who does not believe that they will go someplace elsc after their body expires.  But, if the body, whom you believe that you are, dies, and is buried, then *who* will go someplace else?

If the mind is in, and of the brain, as many of us may believe, then the mind must also die, because the brain, being an organ of the body, must die with the body.

What else is left?  The soul?  Who knows the soul?  Who communicates with the soul?  Who feeds the soul, or even give thought to his soul?  What is the soul without the mind?  It seems that we are lost in knowledge about our life on earth, and, our after earth.

But let us look at this. We connect with our mind more than with anything or anyone else. We spend almost every waking moment communicating something to it or receiving something through it.

We go off at times, to be alone and communicate with mind.

We feed our mind with new knowledge.

We decipher with our mind to get understanding.

And most of all, we trust our mind in guiding us through any and every situation we may get ourselves into.

Right now, we are speaking from the body to the mind, because this is the way we think life is  Think about this: If our body expires, and we still remember who we are, who our family members are, where we are, and the fact that we have left the body, then all information has to be in the conscious mind, and not the brain.

It is the conscious mind that continues to live after the body expires. This means that we are not the body, but we are mind. We are total consciousness. Our bodies are simply vessels that we use to experience what we think. We think, therefore we imagine reality the way we think that it is.

So, if all information, thoughts, and ideas are in the mind, what makes us think that when the body expires, the person is dead?  This is the way we have been conditioned to imagine our lives.  And it is for this reason of believing that we are fleshly bodies, that we are subject to the maladies of the physical or imagined life, i.e. pain, sickness, weariness, lack, etc.

For the record, the mind was originally called the spirit, and the soul was considered the conscious mind, after the body was formed.  It was considered the total awareness.  But due to evolution of our language, we find ourselves getting confused in trying to find a place for all the different nomenclatures, which are really, all the same.

But, in getting back to true reality; there is only God.  He is Spirit; he is Mind.  The Almighty is 100% consciousness.  As we said earlier, that One, is of a multitude of personalities.  Each of these personalities are gods themselves, and together they are the Almighty God. This makes all of them spirit; mind; consciousness.

When each of these personalities decided to form a human in their imagination and like unto the way they see themselves to be, it was mind imagining himself as man.  The difference between this mind and the Almighty was that this mind was individual personalities of God, and the Almighty was every personality.

This means that while every personality was of the One Mind, in effort to express themselves as individuals, they separated their awareness from the oneness. They became conscious and subconscious mind.

The conscious mind, which is the awareness, was the mind that expressed itself through the imagining of a human body. This became the living soul, the objective mind. This child was born from the individual personality of the Whole. His purpose is to experience himself/herself as the being they imagine themselves to be. They were given all dominion, and nothing was limited to them.

The subconscious mind, which remained within the conscious mind, was the subjective mind. This is the part of the mind that provides an experience of every expression.

The subconscious also remains one with the Whole. It is, therefore, the Spirit of the Whole. In Christian terms, this would be the Holy Spirit.

There is another Christian term called eternal life. If man has eternal life, then he is not the body that expires. So, he must be the mind. There, we have evidence that we are minds. All memory is in mind, and mind is eternal.

This means that there is nothing outside of us. But inside of us is a projection of what we have imagined as our bodies and the universe. We simply think, and our thoughts are replicated into our reality.

You might ask, if this is so simple, why is there so much turmoil and chaos in the world?  This is because most people are unaware of the process.  We have been conditioned by life handed down from yesteryear when man was without the help of the subconscious mind.

How can this be?

From the very beginning, represented through the story of Adam and Eve, there is the account of the separation of conscious mind and subconscious mind.  It was not called subconscious mind at that time, but rather, the Garden of Eden.  This is where the life of the individual personality of God was represented as fruit trees.

If the conscious mind (the awareness; the human) allowed for the production of fruits from this garden, he would be expressing the personality within, and receiving its benefits.  This personality was the subconscious mind which was one with the whole, and the Father of the mind within the human.

Scripture tells us that there was a tree in the garden forbidden to eat from.  This was the Tree of the Knowledge of Good and Evil.  To eat from this tree was a choice man would make to be shut off from the guidance of the Garden (Grace) and be led by his own understanding of what was good and what was evil. Man chose to eat from this tree and was therefore, ousted from the garden, and blocked from re-entry by an angel with a flaming sword.  The garden was not removed, man was just blocked from re-entry into this paradise.

From this point until the ascension of Christ Jesus, man lived by his awareness only.  This was by what was physically sensed by him.  This was limited to his surroundings.  So, he lived by his instinct, by habits, by his brute strength; causing him to evolve and lock into the fight or flight mode.  He was as a beast.

He constantly warred with his brethren, and forcefully took the things he thought would give him life.

When mankind became weary with this way of life, he called on God for rescue, salvation from this carousel of misery.  God then, instructed Moses to build a tabernacle of which design He would show him while they were in the wilderness.

This Wilderness Tabernacle that God had Moses to erect during the exodus was a representation of man as the temple of God.  There were three courts to this temple. The outer court represented the flesh of man.  The inner court represented the soul or conscious mind of man. And the inner-most court represented the Spirit of God, also known as the subconscious mind; the Garden of Eden; Paradise.

However, while this inner-most court was in man (the temple), it was shut off from him by a thick red veil without a doorway, representing the blocked path of man back to the Garden of Eden.  The subconscious mind was concealed from the conscious mind. (Man was cut off from God.)

So, at that time, man could not live by purposely projecting his desires into the subconscious mind to get a return of the desired effects. He had no personal contact with the Father. He could only hope for the best, as he attacked the things he unknowingly imagined as his life. Other than that, he had to obey the laws to get the favor of God.

Since then, Jesus has come to pay for man's redemption with his death on the cross, and this opened the communication between conscious and subconscious again.

At Jesus' death on the cross, he proclaimed that the work he had come to do was finished. He, like Moses who was sent to free up God's people and bring them into the Promised Land, was sent to free up the world and bring them into the kingdom of God. (Which is *our* Promise Land) *"For God so loved the world that he gave his only begotten son that whosoever believeth in him shall not perish but shall have everlasting life."* John 3:16.

According to scripture, when Jesus died, his spirit left his body on the cross and went into the Holiest of Holy chamber of the temple. It ripped into two, the veil between the two chambers, and caused them to become one chamber. Conscious and subconscious were married, and once again, one body. On this wedding night, man, who is the bride of Christ, was impregnated with the life that was hid in Christ. Therefore, he aspires, he dreams, he sets goals, he expresses in a certain way, to get a desired effect or experience.

This is the way mind works: The subconscious mind is on the inside of the conscious mind. In fact, the conscious mind is sent forth from the subconscious.

This conscious mind is made up of faculties. Among them are, thinking and reasoning, will, memory, intuition, perception, and imagination. These are the tools that man uses to build his life. When he is sure that what he is thinking is what he believes, then it is released to the subconscious mind for creating the experience of what the man expresses.

The conscious mind is (more or less) the boss. It controls what gets into the subconscious mind for creating. The subconscious mind is a garden. It does not choose or judge what is to be planted there. This is why Adam was instructed to dress the garden. It simply causes whatever seed planted there to grow to its fullest. In other words, a poison ivy plant will grow just as healthy as a stalk of corn.

Since it *is* the life of the conscious mind. This part of the duo guards against anything getting sown there that is not its personal beliefs. Nevertheless, there are many things in this garden that the man, who is the mind, is not satisfied with. This is because there are ways through and around the consciousness that unwanted things can get in.

Some of these ways are through brain washing, and repetitiously having to do something you hate to do, or do not like. Hypnosis is also a way of bypassing the conscious mind to get in. This is because this boss is not as alert or awake as it would like to think that it is. In the 13th chapter of Matthews, scripture talks about a man who planted good seeds in his garden, but while he was asleep (not in vigilance), an enemy came and infiltrated his wheat field, adding tare.

There is a state of consciousness which lies between fully asleep and fully awake, called the Theta state. This is the most vulnerable state for the subconscious mind. Anything or anyone can take control of the subconscious through this doorway. The conscious mind is at rest during this time, while the subconscious is fully awake.

This is the state that Hypnotists have learned to put man into, before taking over the subconscious mind. When man reaches this state, almost any foreign suggestion will become his reality; at least, for a while. Therefore, Therapists suggests affirmations being played in your hearing while you fall asleep, and as you are sleeping.

Even though you cannot consciously hear them after you fall asleep, they are still being received by the subconscious mind. It never sleeps. Therefore, you keep breathing while you are sleeping. This is also why your heart continue to pump blood, and your digestive tract continues to do its job.

You see, your conscious mind, after being nudged by a thought, or after having sensed something in the physical, must pass it through its faculties to form a unanimous decision to what it believes about this thing before expressing. When this decision is made, most times within in a millisecond, it is expressed to the subconscious part of the mind as the flow of life.

The job of the subconscious mind is to deliver this belief to the brain, which is the motor of the body. The brain, with its billions of neurons, will spark signals from one neuron to the other. These sparks will create a temporary neurological pathway which causes the brain to secrete chemicals that will cause the illusion of experiencing the reality that one is believing. (According to science.)

Now, if there is a constant input of the same belief over a certain period of time, the neurons which previously sparked, will begin to form a pathway, or bridge, to ensure a permanent connection for this information being sent to the brain. These roadways are called "Habits".

Once this habit is made, it becomes one of the trees in the Garden of Eden. One does not have to think about this to put it into operations. It has become a permanent part of his life. It will have become the person himself. If it is a habitual thought of joy, this will be a joyous person. And in the same manner, if the habitual thought is sickness, the person will be a sickly person. Therefore, good affirmations and good habits are always admonished. Even scripture says in Philippians 4:8, *"Finally brethren, whatsoever things are true, whatsoever things are honest, whatsoever things are just, whatsoever things are pure, whatsoever things are lovely, whatsoever things are of good report; if there be any virtue, and if there be any praise, think on these things.*

This assures us that life was created to be built deliberately. This is why the church was created. And even if one expressed outside of a deliberate act, he should be sure that it is temporal, and will soon pass. Or it can be changed by the renewing of the mind.

# LIFE IS NOT A GAMBLE

Life is not a gamble; and was never meant to be a gamble. Everything was created to ensure that Elohiym would continuously, and eternally, enjoy the experience of life. Life is the process of expressing oneself and experiencing those expressions.

Isaiah 46:9-11 says, *"Remember the former things of old: for I am God, and there is no one else; I am God, and there is no one like me. Declaring the end from the beginning, and from ancient times the things that are not yet done, saying, my counsel shall stand, and I will do all my pleasure. Calling a ravenous bird from the east, the man that executeth my counsel from a far country: yea, I have spoken it, I will also bring it to pass; I have purposed it, I will also do it."*

This passage of scripture is confirming that there are no mistakes in the world. Every experience is the results of an expression. The Father says, I declare the end from the beginning. He is saying that nothing comes on its own. He expresses it, and whatever he expresses, comes to pass.

The universe, as we have constantly and purposely repeated in this book, is not so much a place as it is an instrument.  It was created to give Elohiym the precise experience to every expression he would put out.

Now, let us get a little deeper.  If Elohiym is defined as every personality, and every personality created a man as himself in his imagination, then every man is God.  *"I have said, Ye are gods; and all of you children of the Most High."* (Psalms 82:6)

Jesus answered them, *"Is it not written in your law, I said, ye are Gods?  If he called them gods, unto whom the word of God came, then scripture cannot be broken."* John 10:34-35

The most heinous mistake a person can make is to think of himself as separated from God, or even a particle of God.  A star is a particle of God, a tree is a particle of God, an animal is a particle of God, but man is a personality of God.  This is God himself.

He says, He calls a ravenous bird from the east, and a man from a far country to execute his counsel.  Since Almighty God is omnipresent, he is everywhere, and there is no East to him; neither is there a far country; they are equally one in him.  But, because he speaks from a place not in the East, and not in the country where the man is, he is evidently speaking from the perspective of a man whose presence is not everywhere.

Scripture is clueing us to the fact that we are the ones who call those things that be not as though they were.  We are the ones that orders the happenings throughout the world.

Understand that, since there is only God, then God created everything for himself. He created life. This was for himself since there was no one else. Therefore, He calls himself "The Living God". In order to express himself and experience the results of those expressions, God took five days to create the instrument that would answer his every expression. This was the universe. Then he took another day to create man in whom he would live this life through.

This means that God as man, and the universe, goes together. This is God's equipment to have life through. Every man is a different personality and Lord God of his own life and his own world. Each man has dominion over everything that happens in his life. His only problem is that he has been conditioned not to believe this, despite its obviousness.

The thing that the man must understand is that his dominion is real, even if he does not believe it. When he speaks, the universe is at his command. He speaks, and the universe speaks in the ear of the ravenous bird, "Go from the East to that certain place"; and the bird, being a part of creation (made just for man), must obey.

The bird was formed by the imagination of man just for this specific purpose.

Ever notice that people coming into your life is but for a season. When you have gotten everything you need from them, to fulfill a certain part of your purpose, they disappear.

Even if it is your best friend or favorite cousin; they are no longer valuable to you, and can disappear, even while still in plain sight. While you still love them, and claim them as your best friend, you can no longer identify with them. You can move on without regrets. Their only worth now is a periodic reunion celebration.

There is nothing wrong with this; you are the avatar of God and is only here to experience the good pleasure of your expressions. Since there is only you, then these people are only here for the makeup of the experience you expressed.

Our problem is that, we get caught up trying to satisfy people, rather than putting out a true, and honest, and purposeful expression. We tend to forget about our purpose, and spend our time trying to deal with our imagination of what the people are thinking.

If each trip man makes into creation is but for the short period of 85 to 100 years, then we have not given ourselves very much time to be sidetracked. Our expressions hold more importance than we may think or believe. This is our life.

Since nothing is without purpose, our being here deserves the utmost attention. Why *are* we here? The dominate belief is that God put us here to meander on this earth until we die, with the only requirements being moral goodness; not to mention, worshipping Him.

In addition, we are under the belief that if we are good enough, we will go to Heaven after we die. If not, we will make our beds in Hell.

The other belief is that we were formed by some accidental chemistry makeup caused during the Big Bang. There, we definitely have no purpose, but to meander here on earth until we die. If any of this is so, then it is no wonder why we believe that life is a gamble.

This indeed, *is* a gamble, if this belief were truth. But no matter how much we are conditioned to believe this, there is nothing created to support it, and nothing that is without purpose. We need warmth, light, nutrients, seasons, and whatever else the sun provides. If these are our needs, then the sun was created to supply those things. It has a purpose. In fact, all the universe is purposed to serve its host, the Lord; in whatever form He chooses to be.

So, if the universe was created for the specific purpose of providing us with the life we express, then our lives were meant to be built deliberately. We express who we are, or what we have, and the universe gives us the experience of those expressions. This is why the Hebrews were ordered to put bread on the Shewbread Table. You must bring what you want to get what you want.  And the universe must answer your expression with like experience.

This is life, and there is no gamble in operating this way. By expressing who we are being, we leave the universe with no guess work.  You call the shots by thinking, acting, and genuinely expressing the emotions of the life you desire to experience.  The universe then, is guaranteed to render unto you, everything it takes to give you the perfectly matched experience of your expression.

But beware; the universe was not created to answer your needs; it was created to give you the experience of the life you express.  If you express need, you will only get that taken away from you which you do have, in order to give you the experience of being the needy person you are expressing.

In all actuality, there really are no needs in the world. There was only one need.  That need was for God to become the Living God.  He created everything for this purpose, and now this need is met.  Absolutely everything else is expressing for life's experiencing.  If someone believes they have a need, it is not really a need, it is simply the experience of their expression.

Surely, they will feel it and be affected by it because this is an experience.  All the senses, including emotions are involved here.  But if one were to renew his mind to express being wealthy, with the same fervor he expressed the need, then the universe has no recourse but to render unto him that experience of wealth instead.

Now, understand that if the universe was created to supply experiences to meet your expressions, then life is not about things, it is about being. In order to have an effective life, one must work on being rather than getting. Getting is the after effect of being. Without being, one cannot receive anything. The universe would have no self-expression to render an experience to.

It has become the common practice in the world for one to express himself according to his/her possessions. Our self-esteem floats according to this perception. When our possessions are low, our self-esteem is low. When our possessions are greater, our self-esteem becomes greater. The problem with this perception is that, even though our self-esteem seems greater, when in the company of people whose possessions are far greater than yours, your feeling of greater diminishes to its previous state of lowliness without anything having changed.

Then, there is the right way!

The thing to always remember is that you are not working on becoming. This is laboring, and you were not created for labor. You are being who you desire to be in your mind and in your heart.

When you are in this place, you are one with all that you are. This is being "Holy". Whether you know it or not, you are in the place of great wealth.

But here is where the problem kicks in. "Ego" will always try to intervene. We have the propensity to want to show off or go beyond who we are being; and there are no provisions for that. Your ego is not who you are. It is who you wish you were, and therefore an expression of poverty in that state. Then, when you cannot see the results of what you want, you begin to doubt. When you begin to doubt, your emotions kick in, changing who you are being, thus, sending out a new expression to the universe. This, in answer, will render a new effect. Probably not so pleasant.

The fact is: All things are yours. When you are being someone (in particular) the universe is obligated to freely give you everything it takes to fulfill the office of that being.

Let us say for instance, you need a new suit to compliment who you are being. While the suit may not fall from the sky, it is already yours. It belongs to who you are being. If someone does not bring it to you, you can buy it out of your present income without ever causing a change in your regular routine which make and keep you who you are.

This is a truth that the world does not understand. Ephesians 1:3, is saying, "You are blessed with all spiritual blessing in heavenly places (The state of mind in which you dwell) in Christ Jesus.  Everything you need to maintain that state is already yours and waiting to serve your needs of being who you are.

As you grow in the being that serves you, your spiritual warehouse grows and changes, to meet every possible thing you will need to maintain the person you are genuinely being.

So, you see, life is not a gamble; it is simply experiencing what you express.  Change your expression and your experience will change.  *"And be not conformed to this world, but be ye transformed by the renewing of your mind…"* (Romans 12:2)

# I AM THAT I AM

Exodus 3:13-15 reads, *"And Moses said unto God, Behold, when I come unto the children of Israel, and shall say unto them the God of your fathers hath sent me unto you: and they shall say to me, What is his name?  What shall I say unto them?  And God said unto Moses I AM THAT I AM: and he said, thus shall you say unto the children of Israel, I AM hath sent me unto you.  And God said moreover unto Moses, thus shalt thou say unto the children of Israel, the Lord God of your fathers, the God of Abraham, the God of Isaac, and the God of Jacob hath sent me unto you: this is my name forever, and this is my memorial unto all generations."*

The same Lord God of Abraham was the Lord of Isaac, as well as Jacob, and the children of Jacob.  This was under the Old Covenant, and each individual person was not given the Holy Spirit whereby they may live as their own individual personalities, as in the New Covenant.  According to God, they were one body, uniformed in the purpose that the Lord had created them for.  For this reason, He was called the Lord of Host.  That is, the one Lord over all the house of Israel.

This is an area of understanding that most Christians are not familiar with.  We try to combine the two covenants into one Bible belief, and are therefore, trying to live them together. Nevertheless, they are 100% different. The Old Testament is of the Law and the New Testament is of Grace. The Law was for every Jew as one, but Grace is for the individual.

The law did not pertain to the Gentiles, because they were not under that covenant. The covenant the Gentiles came in under was Grace. This was the New Covenant which pertained to John 3:16. This was for the world. Scripture says that the Law came by Moses, but Grace and Truth came by Jesus Christ.

Understand that the Old Testament was a shadow of things to come, but the New Testament is the actual appearing of those things which were to come, the truth. 1Corinthians 13:10 says, *"But when that which is perfect is come, then that which is in part shall be done away with."*

The Lord also speaking in Hebrews 8:7-11, says, *"For if the first covenant had been faultless, then should no place have been sought for the second. For finding fault with them, he saith, Behold, the days come, saith the Lord, when I will make a new covenant with the house of Israel and with the house of Judah: Not according to the covenant I made with their fathers in the day when I took them by the hand to lead them out of the land of Egypt; because they continued not in my covenant, and I regarded them not, saith the Lord. For this is the covenant that I will make with the house of Israel after those days, saith the Lord; I will put my laws in their mind and write them in their hearts: and I will be to them a God, and they shall be to me a people: And they shall not teach every man his neighbor, and every man his brother, saying, Know the Lord: for all shall know me, from the least to the greatest."*

Scripture is saying here, that in the New Covenant, no one shall have to teach his neighbor or his brother to know the Lord or what He wants of them. Everyone will know Him, because he speaks to them as individuals now, through his Grace. Because of the shed blood of Jesus, every one of them is empowered to be enjoined to his own personality which is hid in Christ. And so, the Bible says, to be circumcised, or to live by the law, is to deny Christ.

We have the Holy Spirit as our Helper now, and *"As many as are led by the Spirit, they are the sons of God."* (Romans 8:14)

Now understand that the Old Covenant is passed away, and the New Covenant is in full effect now. Nevertheless, while it was mentioned in the history of the Old Testament, the name of God, I AM THAT I AM, is still in effect for this New Covenant. It is not passed away with the Old Covenant. It is not a part of a covenant. He told Moses it would be his memorial unto all generations.

What is the significance of this name, and what does it mean to us now?

As we have learned, God is one. This One is the makeup of every personality that exist. Anything outside of this group would be a god unto itself.  And scripture says, "There is no God beside me."

When God said, "Let us make man in our imagination, after our likeness", every personality that is God, created a person like unto the way they imagined themselves to be, male and female.  Therefore, there is no person alive who is not God, living in His imagination.

Since the name of God is, I AM THAT I AM, then every person's real name is I AM.  Ephesians 3:14-15 says, "*For this cause I bow my knees unto the Father of our Lord Jesus Christ, of whom the whole family of heaven and earth is named.*"

Now, let us say that I AM is the sir name of every person. Then the sir name would be first, in the manner of the Orientals; and the last name would be the individual identity of the person.  This would make "I AM" your family name, and "THAT I AM", your individual personality, or identity.

Now, whenever anyone is asked to identify themselves, their first words are I AM.  This is an automatic indication of your authority.  This is the family name. This is your influence in the universe; and there is no name above this name.  Scripture even admonishes us not to use this name for vanity.

The second part of the name individuates the person.  I am Ivory and my sister is Sedonia.  We are both Ledets, but our individual identity lies in our first names. In this same manner, when we say I am, we are identifying ourselves as a part of a certain influence, but when we finish the statement we are seen clearly as individuals.

In the Old Testament the children of Israel were one body under one Lord, and the rest of the world was considered Gentiles: out of the commonwealth of Israel. However, in the New Testament, the blood of Jesus redeemed every man from the curse of death. Each individual is given the opportunity to be enjoined to his true identity once again, which is his life that is hid in Christ.

Now the six days that Elohiym worked to prepare the universe for his eternal life experiencing, brought it to a completion. The seventh day brought Him into eternal rest. Since every man is a personality of Elohiym, then this Rest was for every man.

This meant that since everything is already done, then the only labor would be to enter that rest and stay there, until your identity is complete.

That labor is to assume the fullness of belief; that is the thought, action, and emotions of the person you desire to be, or to the completion of the I AM of your profession. You do not have to create anything or earn anything. All the honor, the goods, and the glory, is already prepared to overtake any person, for any spiritual place they may be in life.

*"Blessed be the God and Father of our Lord Jesus Christ, who hath blessed us with all spiritual blessing in heavenly places in Christ."* (Ephesians 1:3)

So, whenever you sincerely use the term I AM, you are beginning to identify yourself. Whatever the next words are, activates the pool of God's rest. Your authority as I AM will cause every knee to bow before you and render anything needed to make the experience of your identity a sure thing in this universe.

Should you be cautious? Yes!

Understand that the universe does not unfold against you. It unfolds for you, according to who you have identified yourself as, in your belief and actions. Therefore, I AM, is indicating that you are speaking deliberately. And the universe will deliberately give you the true experience of your beliefs and thoughts. It has no other recourse, and nothing else to do, but render unto you the service it was created to render.

This calls for a focus on the lifestyle you desire to live. Not just the changing of a thing or two, but an exchange of the life you are living for the one you desire.

To think that all it takes is a simple change or two, you are sadly mistaking. That is why diets rarely work. Most people who lose weight by simply dieting, will eventually gain it all back. Why? The reason that they are dieting is because the lifestyle they are living in their mind got them to the place where they need to lose weight.

And even if they do successfully reach their targeted weight, unless there is a change of mind about who they are, their mind set will bring them right back to the weight that is perfect for the I AM they're expressing.

So, your family name, "I AM," is the name that scripture says is above all other names; and at that name every knee shall bow. The universe will not, and cannot, do anything other than deliver unto you the experience you are commanding in your identity of yourself.

Finally, scripture says that the word of God is alive and powerful, and sharper than a two edged sword, piercing even to the dividing into two of the soul and spirit, and of the joint and marrow, and is a discerner of the thoughts and the intents of the heart.

Since scripture also says that all things were created by the Word of God (your words), then we can be sure that it is the word of God working in the Field of Creation (Universe). This means that in the Field of Creation your word is alive, powerful, and sharp, and is able to distinguish between your common thoughts, and the ones that are the intents of your heart. In other words, in the deepest part of you, you know exactly what your words are saying, even if it does not match your intent.

While continuous faking or pretending is one of the best ways of creating a belief or an intent, the universe is still able to discern between the two and will only give you the experience to the degree of your belief. Therefore, scripture says that you are blessed with all spiritual blessings in the place where you are in belief; (mind) "heavenly places".

The universe is the perfect instrument; and it cannot be fooled. Many experts will tell you that you can fool the universe. No, you cannot. But you can fool yourself. It is not the universe's belief that gives you your life experience, it is your belief. The universe will render unto anyone, the experience of the I AM. That is what it was created for.

*"As a man thinketh in his heart, so is he."* (Proverbs 23:7). "I AM THAT I AM"

# MAKE GOOD HABITS

Scripture says, in Hebrews 4:11a, *"Let us labour therefore, to enter into that rest…"* To labor to enter one's rest, is to create habits.

It is a fact that everyone lives by their habits unless you are in the process of creating new habits; then you are living deliberately.

Whether you know it or not, at all times, we are either creating or reinforcing habits in everything that we continuously do. Our habits are stored in the subconscious mind. They create certain neurological pathways in our brains which allows free travel of the chemicals that creates the illusions that we live in. They are the trees which produces the fruits of our living. Proverbs 18:20 says, *"A man's belly shall be satisfied with the fruit of his mouth; and with the increase of his lips shall he be filled."*

What is meant by this statement is that, our lot in life is determined by our habitual lifestyle.

A habit, by being formed in the subconscious mind, puts you in the state of rest. This rest is the Rest of God that we have been referring to. In this rest, no one must struggle to obtain the benefits of his being. This is the rest which has already produced the fruits of it. A habit is like a tree of the Garden of Eden, the fruits are already produced; they make themselves available to you wherever you are. Because where you are is by habit.

The problem with this is that so few people understands it. In fact, habits flow so automatically and freely, that we, most times, fail to realize that we are acting. To be in habit is to be at rest. No one struggles with a habit. Habits are our comfort zones.

Comfort and rest are synonymous.

Unless you are uncomfortably creating a lifestyle for yourself in the Field of Rest, then you are comfortably living from your habits.

Habits are a wonderful thing; this is God's idea of rest. But habits can also be detrimental to your life and living if you do not understand their purpose and operations. Most people have no idea of the importance of habits in our lives.

You see, habits are the fuel of the machinery that runs the Laws of the Universe. Dr. Wernher von Braun, the father of space technology in America, said that the laws of the universe are so precise that we can put a rocket on the moon, in the exact place that we want it, and within seconds of the time projected.

He also said that an electron is materially inconceivable, yet measurable, and because we are familiar with its habits, we can use it to light a city, or to guide an aircraft through the night skies, and even take the most accurate measurements.

The laws are habits and habits are laws. Everything works by habits, and everything is fed by their habits, and everything is predictable by their habits. This is what makes them laws.

Now, man being the imagination of God as himself, also lives by habits. But because our habits can be changed by environments, most of us rarely realize that our lifestyles are nothing more than habits that we have inadvertently made. And the lifestyle the person is living produces the fruits that determines his range of happiness or misery.

If you are automatically experiencing problems and other things in your life on a regular basis that you are not happy with, and if the only choices you have are the best of a group of bad things, then it is assured that you have habits that were inadvertently created in your life. They were created by you, but more than likely through your environment. You have been conditioned by your work, your school, your family, your friends, and yes, even your church.

Everyone sees you, and loves you, and respect you as a peer, but no one knows the real you.  Unless you are actively expressing yourself as who you know that you are, or who you desire to be, even those who love you will presume that you are like them, or they will lovingly make you who they think you ought to be.  And, if you continuously accept and adhere to their way of thinking, you will have inadvertently made habits of an unwanted lifestyle.

Let us look at this thought a little deeper.  Scripture says, "Do unto others as you would have you do unto you." Remember that this is your world, your dream. Everyone that is of any significance in your life is summoned to you by your thoughts and emotions. They were sent by the universe to be a help to you in fulfilling your purpose.  I am remembering, at the time I chose to go into Christian Ministry, my wife and I lost all our friends.  Those who believed me, disagreed with the change, and left.  Those who did not believe me would not acknowledge the change; they continued to treat me the way they thought I should be, for their sake.  We left them.

Now we were without friends anywhere, and we wondered where we would find new friend that would be like minded.  But the very first day I began attending the Seminary, I was greeted by a young minister who happened to be the President of the Student Body.  This young man, who was soon to become my best friend, treated me as if I were already a certified Minister of the Gospel; on the first day.  Not only did he recognize and respect my aspirations, but he treated my dreams as if I had already accomplished them, which point of confidence, I myself had not yet reached, even though I was attempting to portray it.

He saw me as who I was aspiring to be, and pushed me beyond that, making it a must for me to live deliberately. I could no longer live by my old habits, but because he treated me as who I was aspiring to be, I had to deliberately walk the new life until it became a habit for me.  This is what I needed, and this is what my expressions brought me.

In return, I respected him highly in the office that he held, also as a friend, but moreover, I respected and treated him as the model Man of God; whom he still portrays.

This is what he exuded in his actions toward me.  I could not help but give him the same gift that he gave me.  His habits made him respect who I was being, and it was impossible not to respect him.

Now, what was happening here was the fact that, without realizing it, I called this new friend unto me; and I believed that his needs summoned me unto him also. We were able to reciprocate with each other, the exact things each of us needed to become the person we were aspiring to become.  We were of value to each other.

Almost immediately, he and his wife became the best friends my wife and I has ever had.

Now, once again, if you do not know who you are, or you are not showing who you are in your actions, no one can give you the respect or treatment of being anyone special. But they will give you who they choose to make you according to the old habits you are unaware that you are introducing yourself with.

It was easy for me. When I made up my mind to attend the seminary, the universe already had a prepared life waiting for me there. When I began classes, everyone I met believed that I was aspiring to the Gospel Ministry; they treated as a minister. But when you are not deliberately living who you desire to be, your old habits are leading the way, and what is to be thought of you is no more than that which is obvious in you.

All of this is saying that if you are not being treated the way you desire to be treated, or if you are not getting the benefits that you would like to receive in life, it is because you are not being the person to whom these things belong. There is no justification.

All things are already created in the Rest of God, but they are called forth by your thoughts and emotions. If what you want is not deliberately sent in, then your old thoughts and emotions produces by habits, and this becomes the experience your automatic expressions create.

Almost 100% of the time people are unaware that they are living by their habits.  They introduce themselves to the world with their habits and the entire universe will give them, not what they want, but according to who they portray themselves to be, with their habits.

By these things, it becomes a requirement to examine your habits.  Take the time to think about the way you do certain things in your life.  Does your every action and thought say that you are the person that you want to be known as, to the universe?

Unless you have deliberately built your lifestyle by creating the justifying habits, you are living as the person your environment has conditioned you to be.

Scripture says, *"And be not conformed to this world: but be ye transformed by the renewing of your mind..."* (Romans 12:2)

You need a mind overhaul.  This is life, and life is important enough to take the time to examine and correct it.

You will want to first, determine your desires.  Having a definite chief aim and purpose is your start.  This is the most important thing in the world to you.  Nothing should take precedence over this, not even the threat of death.  If you are not actively living who you desire to be, you are dying anyway.

Once you have decided who you desire to be, then choose to be him or her "NOW". Assume the life of the person you desire to be. Be it today. Do not work *at* it; you are not trying to change your body, only your mind. So, live now, with all the thoughts and emotions you want to constantly feel in this life. For how could you possibly make a habit of something you are not practicing?

Deliberately practice these things long enough to make them habits. Once they become a habitual lifestyle, you will do it as a natural move in life, rather than a deliberate act or reaction. You will no longer labor for life but will walk in it without effort or thought. Your chosen life will run automatically. The necessities and accessories will then come, to uphold, and give honor to this honest expression you are putting out to the universe.

This is called "Justification"; reaping the fruits of the trees you have planted.

What does it cost to invest thoughts and emotions to secure the life that produces them? You are mind, and there is nothing that your imagination cannot produce. Remember, whatever is not created and held in the mind, cannot become a part of your life.

So, since we live by habits, and since our habits puts us into the Rest of God, then make good habits. Persevere and endure and even tweak them, until you make them

exactly what you want them to be.  Then they will make
your life exactly what you desire.

# OPERATING IN THE SPIRITUAL LAWS OF THE UNIVERSE

The universe is an instrument. It is like a gigantic factory loaded with grinding and churning machines at every turn. It is the place where custom lives are being created, tested, and sent out for use. The material being used to create these lives are our thoughts and emotions, and therefore, we are endowed with an unlimited supply of material to build the lives that we desire.

The machines in this factory are spiritual laws. They are easy to trust, because each works only one way, and it works all the time.

These laws have no mind of their own, but, as with other tools and machinery, it will do only what it was created to do, to anything that comes within its operating path.

What we mean by this is that, it works like an oven; it will make a cake from any cake batter you put into it. But it is the batter recipe that fine tunes the outcome.

While all the laws of the universe are extremely important in all that we do, in this book we want look at only the two laws I personally consider the most important in the **Basic Knowledge You Will Need To Become An Effective Player of Life In This New World.** These are, the Law of Cause and Effect, and the Law of Attraction.  By understanding these, you will have grasped the major controlling mechanisms of your life in this Time and Space Continuum.  They are the embodiment of every act you will undertake in life.

Let us first look at the Law of Cause and Effect.

# The Law of Cause and Effect

I have recently determined (for myself) that this is the mother of laws, since mostly all the laws seem to have spun off from this one. This is the law that is described in scripture from the passage which reads, *"Be not deceived, God is not mocked; for whatsoever a man soweth, that shall he also reap."* In other words, whatever you pass through this law will produce the one and only result you can get from what you have sown. We also call this the mother of laws because it is the first law we encounter, in creating the life we will live upon this earth. And the fact that it encompasses all the other laws.

The Law of Cause and Effect is just as it is named; for every cause, every action, there is an effect. In everything that is done, something is affected.

Cause and Effect is not something that happens every now and then. It is a universal law and is always in operation. While the results of this law are sensed through actions, we can see it in total idleness. No cause, obviously, no effect. Nothing happens on its own.

This law of the universe is immutable, and there is no way around it. From the moment you have your first thought, to the moment you lay the last brick, every action is measurable by a universal response called effect.

This, as with all other laws, is accurate. You drop a marble to a wooden floor from hip height, and you will get a certain sound. But if you drop the same marble from the same height onto a tin floor, you will get a totally different sound, or a concrete floor, or a dirt floor. Why? Different recipes. This is what makes this law the perfect tool. Different recipes create different results. Your progress can be measured by each action taken.

In creating the lightbulb, Thomas Edison claims that it took him 1,000 tries before he perfected it. Each new filament, or, (whatever) he would change, was the changing of *cause*. He could always depend on each new cause to create a new effect. Therefore, he kept presenting causes until he got the effect he wanted.

A chef adds and changes ingredients until he gets the recipe that he desires for his prize meal.

Each artist mixes different paints until he gets the perfect shade desired for his canvas.

Without this law, perfection could not be so readily attainable. We would have to settle for *"whatever"*.

If you will notice, this is the general forte of the world. We set our cause, *hoping,* and *wishing,* to obtain a desired effect. But why not express the effect you desire in your daily living, as your cause? Then the universe *will have to* render an effect to match the new cause you are expressing.

This is the way all life was designed to live. In other words, if you live the joy and emotions of having abundance, even though you don't physically see it yet, the universe, by law, must give you the things that will match the expression you're putting out. It must give you something to cause the emotions you are emanating.

This Law of Cause and Effect is Gods fundamental plan for the expressing and experiencing of life in the universe. As we said earlier, nearly every other law is born from this one, and is built upon this foundation.

In scripture, we are warned, *"Be not deceived, God is not mocked; for whatsoever a man soweth, that shall he also reap."* This passage reminds us that while life is available for you to have all the fun you desire, it is not made to be taken lightly. It says, be not deceived, God (Life) is not to be taken lightly. Everything is by law and is made to perform perfectly by giving an exact response to your every expression.

You see, this law does not have a "prank or mistake switch" that you can turn on to do something that you do not really intend to happen, then turn it off again for reality. It works the same way every time, and all the time. Therefore, you are cautioned to know what you are intending before you bring a cause into action.

This is also the key that makes it so good. If you knew how to express yourself, you are guaranteed to have anything you desire.

The basic problem in the world, pertaining to the use of this law, is that we are conditioned by the world not to think. We have flitty minds, fleeting thoughts. It is hard for one to keep his mind where he desires it to be for any significant length of time. Our minds usually flit to something else within seconds.

By this, it is hard to focus on what we desire. It is hard to develop an intentional cause to get and intentional effect. Our causes are usually without deep contemplation and focused execution. It is more like throwing a gnat into the oven, while setting the table for a Thanksgiving turkey dinner.

This law, as with all other laws, calls for your undivided attention. You must deliberately send out the corresponding cause to get the desired effect.

For instance, if your doctor told you that you have cancer, believe me, it did not come on by itself. There was a cause made by you to start or give permission to its growth in you. You did not realize you were planting seeds of cancer; otherwise you would have stopped. But because you did not think, speak, and act deliberately, you created something you did not want.

Now, if you *were* thinking deliberately, your thinking had to be led by your erroneous beliefs, or, by your uncontrolled reaction to stimuli from the world.

When Jesus sent his disciples out to evangelize and heal, and even when Elisha sent his servant on a mission, they warned them to keep their eyes forward (meaning to stay focused), and to speak to no man along the way (don't entertain any other possible influences), and go to do a certain thing.

This is saying that every mission in life is to be purposeful and deliberate.

If you purpose to make an apple pie, you do not throw in pears just because they are in the same bowl. You seek out only apples to be the main ingredient of your purposed dish.

It is the same way with operating in this spiritual law of the universe. If you get the news that you, or anyone you know, has been diagnosed with cancer, you must, with all diligence, contemplate your response before you send it out to the universe with your emotions. Your reaction will be your response to the news. Your response will also be the expression you send out, which will be your cause. The universe is waiting to give you the guaranteed experience and effect to your expression.

What answer do you suppose that this kind of news will make you give? If you say, "I need to get rid of this cancer, or, Lord, help me to get rid of this cancer, you would literally be sincerely asking the universe to give you something to contend with. Control your emotions. Make the decision that the symptoms diagnosed by your doctor must go into remission; it has no home in you. Then do something to initiate its departure.

As we said earlier, cancer is not something that you acquire just because it ran in your family, or because you were in the same room with it.  If cancer runs in your family, you do not have it by heredity, you have it because the direction for life that you made habits of was learned from your family.   If they were worriers, then you probably learned to worry also.

Continuous worrying causes stress, and stress causes your vitals to continuously operate in the fight or flight mode, which puts it at the alert level, your highest operating frequency.  This level put strains on your vital organs that could eventually cause wear out and abnormal cell activity, causing a disease-ment.  Often, this disease-ment in the body is given the name "cancer" which means an uncontrolled division of cells in the body, or abnormal cell activity.  Obviously coming from the stress.

However, when *we* think of the name "Cancer", we never think about a simple disease-ment in the body that can probably go into remission by a simple change of mind about your stressful situation.  We think about it as pain, suffering, and death.  We give life to the cancer of death.

If this is the seed you plant, what do you suppose your crop will be?

It cannot be anything different.  For if the planting of apple seeds brings forth apple trees, then how could the planting of suffering and death bring forth healing and life. Remember, *"Whatsoever a man soweth, that shall he also reap."*

When Jesus went home with Jairus to heal his daughter, there was no magic in him, or with him. Not at one time did he plant seeds of death concerning this twelve-year-old girl. He simply said, *"She is asleep"*. They even laughed at him for this. But he understood the laws of the universe, and if he wanted the universe to give life to this girl, he certainly was not going to plant seeds of death with his words and imagination.

Remember when he received the word that his friend Lazarus was dead, he simply said, "Lazarus is asleep. We are going home to wake him from his sleep. He kept it hopeful.

When he arrived at Jairus' home, he put the mourners out of the room, and called in those who would believe with him. After they had agreed that the child was asleep, he simply took her by the hand and told her to awake and rise from her sleep. And she arose.

There are those who represent the majority, that want you to believe that all the miraculous work of Jesus was by a special heavenly magic. By believing this, healing would be almost impossible to attain. Jesus told his disciples, *"Verily I say unto you, He that believeth on me* (That is, operating in the creative laws of the universe), *the works that I do shall he do also; and greater works than these shall he do."*

When people went to Jesus for healing or for help, he never waved his hand and cried "abracadabra", he said, *"As you believe, so shall it be unto you."* And after they were healed, he said, *"Your faith has made you whole."* It is not about magic, but the seeds of belief.

This means that using the Law of Cause and Effect to get what you want, is not something that will automatically work to your advantage. It is a skill that you must learn and practice in your everyday life. We are conditioned by the world, whose concentration is always centered on the problem, instead of the solution.

Nevertheless, it is not the world's job to teach us how to live in these laws; it is the job and purpose of the church. But instead of teaching us how to use the laws of the universe, this school for saints is teaching them that they are wretched worms, sinners, unsaved and worthless beings who can never obtain perfection. Their blessing is always on the way, but never arriving. Their idea of holiness is always coming up the rough side of the mountain, kneeling down at the cross, and sacrificing this precious life that they were given to <u>live on earth</u>, in attempt to *earn* heaven as a home when this life is over. Not realizing that heaven is not for the dead, but the living. And this life is all that matters. That is why Jesus said that heaven is here now, and already in us. Therefore, he told the poor in spirit, the downtrodden, and those who cry, to rejoice, for theirs is the kingdom of heaven; here and now.

One of the most revealing thoughts concerning the Law of Cause and Effect is that it is the only way anything can happen in this universe. If the earth did not spin as it circles the sun, half of it would never see daylight.

The spinning is the act of causing all the surface of the earth to receive sunlight. If your only thoughts would be how to get rid of your sickness, how to come out of poverty, how to find happiness, or any other problem you may think that you have, you will never experience the effects of the opposite side; I am whole, I am wealthy, or I am happy.

**Secret**: All of this is saying, for *every* CAUSE, there is a corresponding EFFECT. For every expression, there is an experience. This is not made to be a special answer to your special problem; this is simply the way of life for every living soul. Remember, our bodies are only a sensed image or projection of our thoughts about ourselves. The only thing that could happen in our bodies is what we first cause from our thoughts.

Whatever you think, believe, or do, is an expression which is *causing* the manifestation of a corresponding experience or effect. For every cause, there is an effect. The creation of every effect is in response to every cause.

So, while you are thinking about how to get rid of your sickness, you are causing the universe to give you a sickness that you will always be trying to get rid of.

While you are wishing for and trying to get money, the universe will bless you with the need for money.

This is what you are expressing.

Now, stop and think about this statement again. For every cause, there is an effect. And every effect stems from a cause.

We have not been taught to use this law correctly. For if the cause to fight sickness brings on more sickness, and the cause to overcome poverty brings on more poverty, then it is the energy we put out that is at work. This means that the law is accurate, but it is being used backward.

Why not reverse it? Use it the way it was created to be used. You create the effect you want by living it, then let the universe present a cause to that effect. It must!

If you have been diagnosed with, or you are feeling sick, then act and believe the effect you desire. First, become what you desire to happen in your life. Naturally, you cannot do it in your body. Your body can only reflect your mind. So, do it in the mind. Live it as if you already had it. This will become your cause. And if this is the cause you present, then the only effect the universe could possibly create for you are the things that would justify your cause.

You must cultivate and live by the belief that you can get up and walk whenever you will choose to, even though the world believes that you are permanently confined to your wheelchair.

Remember, your emotion is the cause the universe is dealing with. The universe is not considering, or dealing with your money, it is not dealing with your needs, nor is it considering your doctor, or even other people; it is dealing with *your* beliefs only.

If you believe and act happy, the only thing the universe can render to you are the things that you believe can make you happy.

If you believe and are expecting to be healed from your sickness on a certain day, or by a certain act, when that day come, or after you perform that certain act (with belief), the universe has no recourse but to render the effect of your belief.

Why has this never happened to you before? It has and is happening all the time. Your problem is the recipe of your belief. If you put out the emotions of the belief that you are sick, even though you desire to get well, the universe can only read your emotions. If you believe that you are poor and must pinch pennies, this is the only emotion the universe can read.

However, if you put out the cause that you are wealthy and happy; when you can make a habit of emoting these feelings that you would love to continue having as your reality, then the universe must render unto you, the monetary gifts, and the things that will bring the joy that will justify the way you have been acting.

If you want to remain youthful, quit thinking about how old you are.

If you want it to rain, quit thinking about how dry it is.

Remember: God, our higher self, created the universe for his good pleasure; to give him an experience to everything he would think of himself as being.

If he thinks himself rich or poor, he will experience what he honestly believes. If he thinks himself dumb or smart, he will experience what he honestly believes. Therefore, scripture warns, *"As a man thinketh in his heart, so is he."*

Therefore, it is mandatory that this law be taught and studied diligently in the church and in the home, and not to be taken for granted that you already know. This is the thought of fools. (See Deuteronomy 6th chapter.)

Jesus said, "When you pray (focus or meditate), believe that you are already receiving what you desire, and it shall be yours. What you believe for the present moment, is all the universe has, to deal with. There is no such thing as luck.

What you are hoping for will always remain a hope, and never a possession.

Remember it this way: You are the ruler of the universe in you, and it was created to serve you. Whatever you express is the experience you desire to have. The universe, having no mind of its own, must diligently render unto you the things that will match with what you are feeling and believing.

*"Let the poor say I am rich and let the weak say I am strong."*

## *The Law of Attraction*

The Law of Attraction is perhaps the most popular law of the group. Movies have been made about it, books written on it, and it is being taught by self-help gurus around the world. This law states that whatever you focus your attention on, for any significant length of time, will be drawn into your experience.

This is one of the laws which span from the Law of Cause and Effect. The energy of your focus is the cause here.

Since focus is applied energy, it is always creating in this universal Field of Creation. Ever notice that the things which you try hardest to avoid are those things which eventually makes its way into your experience. This is because the things you try to avoid are the things you are most focused on.

Things you are desiring to have and things you are desiring to avoid are equally powerful in your life, according to the attention you are giving it. Eventually one will outweigh the other, and it will work its way into your life experience.

This law is one of the simplest laws of all to take control of your life through. But the problem with grasping a good understanding of it is with all the baggage that has been attached to it. With all the hoopla being associated with this Law of Attraction, it is a wonder that anyone can understand it.

So, our mission in this chapter is to make it as understandable as it is simple. We will attempt to make it short and sweet for your understanding and knowledgeable usage.

When you understand the basics of how the universe works it will become simple. In talking about how the universe works, we are not talking science or religion, though both are pointing to this. But we are talking about spiritual; something science and religion try to replace rather than incorporating.

Understand that everything began spiritual. God is spirit, and since everything exist from God, then everything we know as creation, or the universe, is also, and predominately spiritual.

Spirit is mind power rather than physical power. Physical is creation, and mind is the creator. We create in our mind; we imagine our lives.

The universe was created as an imagined place where God can express and experience life through. Our biggest problem with this is that we have been conditioned to believe that God and the universe are in two different places, and He would have to come down from the place he resides in to enter the universe.

The plain factual truth is that, for one to be someplace or to do something, it would have to be done somewhere. One cannot be nowhere. One cannot even imagine himself being nowhere. When you cannot associate yourself as being someone somewhere, then it is a fact that you do not exist. But because you think, you exist. And because you exist, you exist as someone, somewhere. That somewhere is in the universe.

As we have so diligently stated and proven in the previous chapters, God is one and that one is the makeup of a multitude of personalities called Lords. Each of these personalities being different, imagined themselves in a particular way. Each imagined a being in the likeness of who they felt themselves to be. This proves a fact that there is no one in existence who is not one of these personalities of God imagining himself as a human being. This also proves the impossibility of anyone existing who is not a god personality.

But now, without a material thought, no personality would have a picture of himself. Neither would he have a picture of a place that he could exist in. So, for God to express himself as who he imagined himself to be, and to experience the being of that self, he had to create a mental universe. Here He could see himself as what he imagined he looked like, in the place where he would imagine himself to be.

This instrument that we call universe is so precise that if he would begin to imagine himself as someone different, the universe would re-configure its position to fit the mind of the being. Therefore, it is called "universe"; it fits all. For instance, if you were to move into an unkempt home, in a ragged and stinking neighborhood, or even in a trash heap, you would probably be miserable for a few days, but as you get used to operating in this place, your mind began to adjust to your surroundings, and you will eventually find comfort there. This is because your environmental conditioning forced a change in you, as mind. And therefore, the place will seem to have changed for you. It would match your conditioning. Your focus would be on where you are.

But this is universe, as God created it. It was created to become anything that the mind would make it, through the power of imagination; seeing it as you believe it is. And different personalities see different things.

Now, on the average, we see things as we have been conditioned to see them. As the old saying goes, "One's junk may be someone else's treasure." All of it depends upon your conditioning or your belief system.

What we focus on is what we believe. No one ever focus on a giant's foot crushing his rooftop, and therefore, we never hear about it in the news. But we focus on the weather, we focus on the traffic, we focus on our fears, and we even focus on our lacks, and these things accommodates us with an appearance like unto our thoughts or beliefs about it. This is called the Law of Attraction.

When we meditate or think deeply, we are focusing our thoughts on one particular thing about any given subject. This focused thought is the energy that is released into the Field of Creation, and the power of this thought gives birth to itself in this field. When we can see it clearly, it is then made real in our lives. This is the power of focus in the universe, and this is God's gift unto himself.

Now, *we* have this power in us as, not only a part of us, but our very being. We cannot separate ourselves from this power of the universe, because without it, we, as we know ourselves, do not exist. Our entire beings are focused thoughts being formed in the field of creation. As we think ourselves, we see ourselves. As we think our possessions, we see our possessions. As we think our circumstances, so they are. No luck and no magic at work here, what you see is what you have created. "As a man thinketh in his heart, so is he."

The gist of the whole matter of creation is this: The universe is a power that is as a projection screen. It only shows what is projected onto it from our beliefs; the focusing of our minds. You cannot see what you do not believe. Since we can only imagine what we believe, then we can understand that we cannot, and do not, focus on what we do not believe.  And you cannot have what you do not believe.

Now, here is where we get down to the grid.  It is quoted of God in scripture, that all things are yours.  But, as with anything at all, if you do not know how to obtain it, you cannot have it.  This is the problem with people making the Law of Attraction work in their favor.

If you desire a thing, but you cannot see any way possible, but by magic, to obtain that thing, you cannot have it; though it is freely yours to have.

As we said, no one can focus on what he does not believe.  Whether you believe it or not, the thoughts that the universe receives from you is not so much the thing that you desire, as it is the results of your beliefs about this thing.

Your thoughts are always based on the effects that this thing will have in your life; how good it will look on your wrist, how great it will taste, how it would make you feel, etc.  These are positive thoughts that are creating in your favor.  But when you do not believe you can have it, you cannot imagine the feel of it on your wrist, or the taste of it.  Your dominant belief and focus are pushing it away from you.  As Jesus said, "When you pray (focus), believe that it is yours, and you will have it."

Most of us are conditioned to believe that we must fix something to make it work in our favor.  This means that we are always looking in the past to secure our future.

The problem with this is that you cannot fix what is already created, you can only acknowledge it as a finished thing and move on.

By thinking that something must be a certain way to obtain what you want, you will always have something standing in the way of your getting good results. For by believing that conditions are not right to get your desired thing, it becomes impossible for you to focus on anything but that problem. And the Law of Attraction states that whatever you focus on will be drawn into your life experience.

So, fight nothing; have a good rapport with all your thoughts. But instead of focusing on the undesirable ones, see them on the opposite pole. Imagine the opposite of what you do not want; but never acknowledge that you do not want it. This will give it the attention it needs to grow, and this is what you really do not want.

So be at peace with yourself. Fear no undesirable thoughts. If you will fear, then fear being overwhelmed with the things that you desire most.

# BECOME A BELIEVER

*"Even so faith, if it hath not works, is dead, being alone. Yea, a man may say, Thou hast faith, and I have works: show me thy faith without thy works, and I will shew thee my faith by my works. Thou believest that there is one God; thou doest well: the devils also believe, and tremble. But wilt thou know, O vain man, that faith without works is dead?"*

For the record, disciples of Jesus Christ were not called Christians until approximately two years after Jesus' ascension.

Up to this time they were called "Believers".

They were called believers because, they had learned from Jesus, the fundamentals of life, as it was meant to be lived here on earth.

As life goes, mostly all of our desires, decisions, and actions, are based upon circumstances we find ourselves having to deal with. And in many cases, they are circumstances that seems to be greater than our capacity to handle them.

But Jesus taught them the little-known secret that circumstance was not their enemy. It was simply the results of what they created from a previous thought or belief.

You see, when circumstances arise, we handle them in a certain way, which is according to our beliefs about our present strengths. The outcome of our actions will render unto us peace, or, the residue of incomplete or botched work.

Let us say for instance, You have a large bill payment on a debt that is overdue, but you are broke. Your action might be to ask for an extension until the next month, or you may borrow the money from someone else to pay it.

Well, the overdue bill was the first circumstance facing you. You handled it through the only strengths or options you believed you had.

Now, a new circumstance was created by your actions.

This new circumstance that your actions created was not "peace". It may have been peaceful for the moment, but while your creditor has been satisfied, nothing at all has changed, but the additional person you are now indebted to, if you borrowed the money. You still owe the money to the person you borrowed it from to satisfy your creditor.

So now, when the next month rolls around you are indebted to two parties rather than the original one.

Had you chosen to ask for the extension, your obligations would be doubled <u>now</u>, what you couldn't afford to pay <u>single</u>, last month. And if this is the pattern of your belief, until something explodes, your entire life will be put on hold, dealing with the rapidly growing circumstances you are feeding. You will never have the chance to live what you desire.

Now understand this! Your circumstances were created by the actions you took concerning a certain thing. The actions you took were based upon your thoughts about the options you had. Your options were based upon what you thought about who you are, what you have, and what you could do.

So here, we find a law that proves that we live by what we believe. This makes belief, the most important thing in the world. Thus, our title, "Become a Believer".

"Christianity" was eventually accepted over "Believers" due to a weakness the term "Believers" had incurred. People had begun to leave off believing for life. Their belief had been reshaped to mean, believing that there is a God, or there is only one God. The same belief that most of Christianity still honors today. But the Apostle James pointed out in his Book, that even the devils believe there is but one God, and it makes them tremble. But, he added, wilt thou know O vain man, that faith is a combination of belief and works? To say you believe, and have no obvious works to support it, means that your faith is dead.

Why is your belief so important?

Belief is all there is.  Everyone believes; either one thing or another, but we all believe.  There is nothing that exist to us without belief.  And the surprising thing about it is that no matter what you believe, your actions will naturally correspond with the dominate thought.  You may not get the results of what you are hoping for, but you will get the results of your beliefs.

As we said earlier, the universe is built upon a foundation of laws.  However, it is "belief" that operates these laws, and bring your life into, what we call, a reality.  When you express your belief, you are creating your life.  The effect of your beliefs becomes your reality.

Belief is power.  We say it is power because, this thing is the fuel that, not only operates the universal laws, but when infused with emotions, will transform you into the exact being you actually see yourself as.

Now, these laws are so precise that it is impossible to find error with them.

The results of belief are accurate because it can only create a picture of you as the person you truly think that you are or see yourself as.  It cannot paint a picture of life and possession around you outside of the way you see your personality.

Though you may desire riches, they are impossible to be visualized as having it, when you can only see yourself as needing it. When you believe that you need it, you are believing that you are poor or without the provisions that you require for life. This then, invokes another law which states, "Unto them that have not, even what do have shall be taken away from them.

There is no hiding place. There is a law to bring into your reality, every thought you pay attention to. The term, "pay attention", is not just a slang. This is the actual act of buying an idea into your belief system.

There is another saying that goes, "Where your attention goes, your energy flows. Your energy is the currency of life. It can only be spent or invested in the Field of Creation; the place where your reality is made.

Believe it or not, all energy is spent on creating your circumstances, which is, at this point, your reality in life.

So, how can this belief, which is keeping us in bondage, be used to give us a more desirable life?

The Apostle Paul's answer to this is found in Romans 12:2, *"And be not conformed to this world, but be ye transformed by the renewing of your mind..."* KJV

It may help to understand that nothing that you call reality is permanent. It is simply your thought for the moment.

At any time, you can spot something, or hear something, that will cause you to believe differently, and instantly, your situation or circumstance has changed. A different belief is all it took.

Now, you may ask, if it is only a thought, why is it so painful? This is because it is an experience. It is what you ordered with your expressions from your belief. And naturally, an experience must be "Experienced". This is why it is called an experience. You sense it with all your physical senses. And your thoughts about what you are feeling creates the emotional effects and scars left, after it is gone.

So, how do I overcome this? Change your thinking; create a new belief about it. Your limited belief, knowledge, and conditioning may not presently contain anything to override this. But this does not mean that there is no salvation for you.

Look around you, do some research. As with Jabez of scripture, "Expand your territory"; "Lengthen the cords of your tent." Increase your knowledge. Find something that you would love to replace this problem with. When you find it, do not ever let this thought go. Learn everything you need to know about it. Plant it in you, as yours already. Then continue to fertilize and water it with additional information from your research that meets your desires. The more knowledge you add to you, the more real it will become to you. The more real it becomes, the less real your circumstance will seem.

Begin to live it like it is yours already. When it becomes a full belief, then circumstance will have to change into the experience of your new expression.

Your present belief is all there is to your life. To change your belief is to change your reality.

Therefore, belief becomes the master of life.

Since belief is created by your thoughts about certain subjects, then, as Paul said, Think on those things that are lovely. No matter how bad a situation may seem, think only, upon the outcome you desire to see.

This is your goal, make it your expression, and it has no other recourse than to become your experience.

The key is this: despite all the possible ways life could go wrong for you, think instead, on the outcome you desire to experience. And understand, there is no power higher than the power of your thoughts.

Think on the life you desire to live, and you will live the life you think about. There are no exceptions; this is the way life works, and the power is in your belief.

You are a child of God, and all power and dominion in your life is yours.

This is where faith is required. Please God by walking in your faith. Remember, belief without works is not faith.

Scripture says, Abraham believed God, and it was counted unto him as righteousness.

The Bible uses many names for God, each of them designed to reflect one facet of His glorious character. In this series, Gaylyn Williams has done a remarkable job of identifying and explaining the various names God uses to describe Himself. Meditating on these names, one day at a time, will help us to know God more intimately. This series will prove useful in enriching one's daily quiet time.

—**Jerry Bridges**, Author of twelve books, including,
*Trusting God Even Though It Hurts* and *The Joy of Fearing God.*

There is no greater means to become free of sin, sadness and sorrow than taking our eyes off ourselves and placing our hope wholly in God. Knowing the names of God is to know the heart of God. Gaylyn Williams helps us know God better by revealing his character and nature. Take the time to read this book and you will be changed.

—**Gary Wilkerson**,
President, World Challenge and Lead Pastor, The Springs Church

It seems our Creator puts a lot of stock in names. I'm sure He knows my name but do I know His? This exceptional daily devotional reveals God's character. What a relationship builder is this guide to all who want to draw closer to God. And when we draw closer to Him, "blessings" happen.

—**Chuck Asay**, Syndicated Editorial Cartoonist

This book is a labor of love from Gaylyn Williams' heart, to God's people who desire to know Him better, and what better way to get to know Him than to study His names. I urge you, to use this book along with your Bible, read it daily, study it and meditate on Him, the God who is Love (1John 4:16). As I studied this book, I often found myself laughing, shouting and crying with joy as the Holy Spirit would overwhelm me with the greatness of Who God is. As I type this, tears of joy fill my eyes again. It is joy over what this has done for me and what Father will do for you, through this work, if you will open your heart and take the time to get to know Him through His names. Wow!!! What a Savior!!!

—**Steven R Sherwood, Sr.** Pastor Fairview Baptist Church, Kokomo, IN

I've always found great joy in exploring God's unique identity and have studied it often. But this book has opened my eyes in new ways to appreciate who He is, and to love Him more than ever. Each day is a heart-warming adventure as I come to know Him more, and examine my relationship with Him in new ways.

—**Ken Williams, Ph.D,** Founder of International Training Partners

Having been a follower of Christ from a young age and then surrendering to ministry as a teenager, I have often found myself in "desert places." Through those dry times, God has always been faithful to water my soul in unexpected ways. "The Surprising Joy of Exploring God's Heart" has been one of those surprises. God has used this book to lovingly bring hope and refreshing back into my heart and home. Through the easy to read format, heartfelt prayers and pointed questions, I have slowed down enough to fix my gaze upon the All-sufficient One. What joy to rest in His presence.

—**Evelyn Sherwood**, Ministry Leader, Minister's Wife, Mom and Grandma

These brief meditations are geared specifically to the contemporary believer's busy life. Gaylyn shares 365 ways God is addressed in Scripture. And she invites busy Christians (me…you) to engage in understanding God more intimately. These brief, to the point page-long meditations and Gaylyn's questions urge the reader toward application to personal life in the 21st Century.

—**Sandra T. Auer**, Campus Crusade for Christ, Member Care

We can never get enough of God nor can we fully comprehend His character. However, Gaylyn's fresh approach to learning and honoring the names of God is a powerful and practical tool for better knowing our Father in Heaven. The unique daily format provides teachings and practical applications that guide the reader into a deeper and higher relationship with the Father. The reader will especially benefit from the daily prayers that encourage greater submission to the Father's will as they develop a better understanding of His nature. This is a nightstand tool, a daily must *read*, and can be used year after year without exhausting your understanding of God.

—**Amy Everette**, Director, Colorado Concert of Prayer

We will never grow beyond our revelation of who God is. Everything in our lives flows from our understanding of the character and attributes of God. One of the best ways to grow in our relationship with God is to grow in our understanding of His names. This book is a great tool to become more intimately acquainted with the many facets of God's character by praying into and thinking deeply upon the names of God.

—**Jayde Duncan**, Senior Pastor of Freedom Church in Colorado Springs